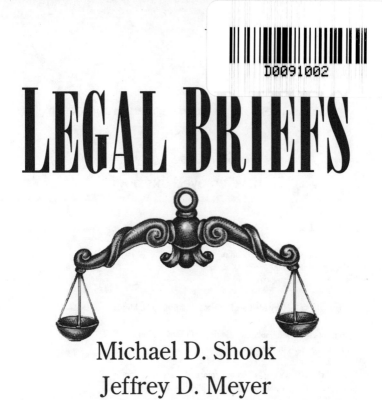

LEGAL BRIEFS

Michael D. Shook

Jeffrey D. Meyer

MACMILLAN • USA

In memory of our beloved grandfather,
Herbert Shook;
a man of immense wit, he would
have enjoyed this book.

MACMILLAN

A Prentice Hall Macmillan Company
15 Columbus Circle
New York, New York 10023

MACMILLAN is a registered trademark of Macmillan, Inc.
Library of Congress Cataloging in Publication Data

Shook, Michael D.
    Legal briefs / Michael D. Shook, Jeffrey D. Meyer
        p.   cm.
    Includes Index
    ISBN 0-02-860042-8
    1. Law—United States—Miscellanea.   2. Law—United States—Anecdotes.
I. Meyer, Jeffrey D.   II. Title.
KF387.S48   1995
349.73—dc20
[347.3]   94-42558   CIP

Manufactured in the United States of America
10 9 8 7 6 5 4 3 2 1

ACKNOWLEDGMENTS

Several people contributed to the publication of *Legal Briefs*, to all of whom we are very grateful. Our agent, Jeff Herman, was inspirational throughout the entire preparation of the manuscript, and we are thankful to him for having secured Macmillan Publishing to publish this book. We also appreciate the guidance, constructive editing, and thoroughness of our editor, Laura Wood.

Jeff especially appreciated the love and support of his wife, Debbie, during the grueling hours it took to create this book. Robert Shook, author of 36 books, provided us with invaluable insight based on his experiences. A special thanks to Maggie Abel for her organizational skills and proof-editing and to Suzette Crawford for typing and editing. Jon Meyer, Karen Meyer, Matt Meyer, Carrie Shook, and R. J. Shook also provided a great deal of support. We also appreciated the help of Murray Davis, Steve Edwards, Jim Kapenstein, Tim Madison, and personnel at Benesch, Friedlander, Coplan & Aronoff. We thank these wonderful people for their assistance and their inspiration; without them, it is doubtful that *Legal Briefs* would have been possible.

A portion of the trivia contained in this book was provided as a courtesy from LEXIS ®/NEXIS ® Services, online legal, news, and business information services with more than 5,000 databases and 580 billion characters online. Over 2.5 million documents are added each week to the more than 475 million documents online. The LEXIS ® Service contains major archives of federal and state case law, continuously updated statutes of all 50 states, and state and federal regulations and public records from major states. The NEXIS ® Service contains major news publications including *The New York Times* and *The Washington Post*, as well as national network and regional television broadcast transcripts and national public radio news and features. For further information, the LEXIS ®/NEXIS ® Services toll-free number is 1-800-227-4908.

CONTENTS

INTRODUCTION

Practically everything in today's hectic world is affected by the law. Your involvement with the law begins on the day you are born, when your birth certificate is legally registered, and it continues until the day you die, when a death certificate confirms your demise. It doesn't stop there, however. If you've ever been named a beneficiary in a will, you're already acquainted with how the law lets no one off the hook, even in the afterlife.

But while there are plenty of complex laws in great tomes, by no means does this suggest that lawyers are a logical breed, nor does it imply that the law itself consists of sound reasoning. On the contrary, as you'll see in Chapter 1, many ludicrous laws abound in the United States. Did you know, for instance, that in Scottsbluff, Nebraska, a law prohibits storing snowballs in a refrigerator; in Oxford, Ohio, a woman is breaking the law if she undresses while standing in front of a man's photograph; and in Hartford, Connecticut, it is against the law to cross the street while walking on your hands? Silly laws know no borders. In India, a woman can legally marry a goat; in modern Egypt, a belly dancer must dance with her navel covered with gauze; and in Switzerland, false teeth are outlawed!

1

Legal Briefs also includes other intriguing information about the law. Did you know, for example, that although the United States has but 5 percent of the world's population, it has 70 percent of its lawyers? In Washington, D.C., there is one lawyer for every 17 people; North Carolina has the fewest per capita with only one lawyer for every 704 residents.

Few characters in any profession are as amusing as lawyers, particularly those who take themselves seriously without the slightest intention of being amusing. But in *Legal Briefs*, the fun we poke at lawyers is without malice, especially as one of us is currently a member of the bar—and endeavors to continue the practice of law for a very long time.

While we anticipate that lawyers will derive the most enjoyment out of this book, few subjects are as generally fascinating as the law, and we hope every reader will enjoy reading about it. If so, we've done our job well. Perhaps you'll want to pass this book along to a friend, fellow attorney, client, or anyone else with an inquisitive mind and a keen sense of humor.

Chapter 1

THAT'S ILLEGAL! DATED, FRIVOLOUS, AND UNNECESSARY LAWS IN THE UNITED STATES

Here is a collection of little-known laws promulgated by courts or enacted by politicians, many of which by today's thinking are frivolous, or worse. Most of them had some significance when they were originally enacted, but have not been overruled or repealed due to legal inertia. Although most of the laws are not enforced, they will still have you shaking your head saying, "Why in the world . . ."

It is against the law in Georgia to slap an old friend on the back.

In Berea, Kentucky, a law still stands that requires a horse to have a bright red taillight securely attached to its rump during the night on the streets and highways.

A fourteen-year-old in Michigan can sue his parents for the right to wear his hair long.

Graffiti has become so prevalent in New York City that it is now unlawful to even carry an open can of spray-paint there.

Carrying a concealed weapon more than six feet long is illegal in Seattle, Washington.

In Salem, West Virginia, it is against the law to eat candy any time during the hour and a half before attending a church service. During this same period, it is illegal to sell candy to a minor.

Dancing—even at a high school prom—is banned in the schools in Purdy, Missouri.

In Shreveport, Louisiana, it is against the law for undertakers to advertise their services by giving away pencils carrying the name of the funeral home.

The law in Cicero, Illinois, forbids humming on the streets on the Sabbath.

It is against the law to do acrobatics that might frighten horses on the sidewalks of Denver, Colorado.

An Abilene, Texas, law makes it illegal to whistle at girls.

You cannot own more than five cats at a time and live within the city limits of Topeka, Kansas.

In Homer, Georgia, only the men on the police force are permitted to carry guns.

Why It's Called a "Sundae"

In the 1880s, laws were passed in Midwestern towns prohibiting the sale of ice-cream sodas on Sunday. In Illinois, fountain owners skirted the law by omitting the carbonated water and serving just the scoop of ice cream and the syrup. They called it a "Sunday soda." Later, "Sunday" was changed to "sundae."

In Geneva, New York, it is against the law to tell an attendant after dark to "fill her up."

It is unlawful in Florida to doze off under a hair dryer.

Storing snowballs in a refrigerator is illegal in Scottsbluff, Nebraska.

In Oxford, Ohio, it is against the law for a woman to strip off her clothing while standing in front of a man's picture.

A law in Franklin, Massachusetts, doesn't permit anyone to wear a turkey feather in a cap or hat.

In Boston, Massachusetts, an ordinance states that any pickle for sale must bounce four inches when dropped from waist height.

School teachers are not permitted to "bob" their hair in Arkansas, and the law specifies that "no pay raises will be authorized to teachers who violate this code."

Cats are not allowed on a bus in Seattle, Washington, if a dog is already aboard. And, any dog weighing twenty-five pounds or more is charged a full adult fare.

Georgia barbers cannot legally advertise their prices in any manner.

It is against the law to open an umbrella in front of a horse in New York City.

In Hartford, Connecticut, it is against the law to cross the street while walking on your hands.

Although watches, diamonds, and silver flatware cannot be auctioned after 7 p.m. in Houston, Texas, the law permits the auction to start again at 4 a.m.

It is against the law to throw snowballs in Oklahoma City, Oklahoma.

In Pontiac, Michigan, taxi cab drivers are not permitted to give a ride to anyone engaged in an illegal undertaking.

You cannot walk down the street with your shoelaces untied in Maine.

A minimum fine of $25 is levied on anyone scaring wild ducks during Michigan's official hunting season.

It is unlawful in Louisville, Kentucky, for businesses to install air-conditioning systems that blow air through sidewalk gratings and lift up ladies' skirts.

In Duluth, Minnesota, it is illegal to let animals sleep in a bakery.

Using the name of a dead United States president to advertise liquor is against Michigan law.

A law prohibits bringing a mule into town and hitching it to a fire-alarm box in Washington, D.C.

It is illegal to read while walking in the street in New York City.

In Green Bay, Wisconsin, it is against the law for a car to drip on the pavement. The fine for this offense is one dollar for each drop.

New regulations in Detroit permit mail carriers to wear Bermuda shorts, but they are required to wear black socks.

If an elephant is left tied to a parking meter in Orlando, Florida, the parking fee must be paid exactly as if it were for a motor vehicle.

In the United States, only the male head of a household is allowed to make wine.

Cab drivers in Albuquerque, New Mexico, are forbidden to reach out and pull prospective customers into their cabs.

A recent California law prohibits offering a "dead or alive" reward.

In New Orleans, Louisiana, biting someone with your natural teeth brings a simple assault charge; however, if you do so with false teeth, it is an aggravated assault.

Car drivers in Detroit, Michigan, are prohibited from carelessly, willfully, wantonly, or recklessly splashing water by driving through puddles.

In Eureka, Nevada, the law reads: "A mustache is a known carrier of germs, and a man cannot wear one if he habitually kisses human beings."

Car wash attendants in San Francisco, California, are barred from using cast-off underwear as wiping rags when cleaning or drying cars.

In Logan County, Colorado, a man is forbidden to kiss a woman "while she is asleep without first waking her."

In Memphis, Tennessee, you cannot give any pie you order in a restaurant to a friend; nor can you wrap the pie in a napkin to take home and eat later. You must, by law, eat every bit of the pie before leaving the restaurant.

Each month, according to a New York state law, theater owners must scrape the chewing gum from under the seats.

It is against the law in California to shoot any kind of game, bird, or mammal, except a whale, from an automobile or airplane.

Barbers in Illinois cannot use their fingers to apply shaving cream to a customer's face.

It is against the law in Utah to fish from horseback.

In Miriam, South Dakota, it is illegal to smoke candy cigarettes in any school.

A Wisconsin law prohibits feeding margarine, rather than real butter, to prisoners.

In Alabama, it is illegal to play dominoes on Sunday.

Peanuts must be eaten where sold in Houston, Texas.

Jazz dancing at any public place is against the law in Savannah, Georgia.

First Speed Law

Boston's Board of "Selectment" enacted America's first speed law in 1757: "Owing to great danger arising often-times from coaches, sleighs, chairs, and other carriages on the Lord's Days, as people are going to or coming from the several churches in this town, being driven with great rapidity, and the public worship being oftentimes much disturbed by such carriages, it is therefore voted and ordered that no coach, sleigh, chair, or chaise, or other carriage at such times be driven at a greater rate than a foot pace, on penalty to the master of the slave, or servant so driving, of the sum of 10 shillings."

It is unlawful in Kentucky to appear in the streets dressed in a bathing suit without police protection.

Gargling in public is against the law in Louisiana.

It is unlawful in Maine to participate or aid in the fighting between rats.

Dragging a rope through any street is prohibited by law in Cumberland, Maryland.

It is against the law for roosters to crow before sunrise in Greenville and Beaufort, South Carolina.

In the city of Mobile, Alabama, it is illegal to fly a kite on any street or public place.

Sleeping in a kitchen is prohibited by law in California, but it is legal to cook in a bedroom.

It is unlawful to use profane language in a telephone conversation in Georgia.

A Kentucky law states that only a female horse can be ridden near a church while services are in progress.

Displaying the American flag in a public park is unlawful in Flint, Michigan.

In Columbus, Montana, an ordinance states that "any person who shall not lift his hat to the Mayor as he passes him on the street will be guilty of a misdemeanor."

It is illegal to drink or make love in a rural churchyard in North Carolina.

Women's wrestling is not allowed in the city of Gloversville, New York.

It is against the law to blow your nose in public in Waterville, Maine.

In Ironton, Ohio, it is illegal to dress up like the opposite sex and appear on the streets.

Wife beaters are not allowed to vote in South Carolina.

It is not considered burglary to steal goods hanging from the outside of a house in Texas.

Sneezing on a train is against the law in West Virginia.

It is illegal to sell lollipops in Spokane, Washington.

Disturbing a grizzly bear to photograph it is prohibited by law in Alaska unless you are accompanied by a registered guide.

Any person washing his hands, face, or feet in a public fountain in the city limits of Mobile, Alabama, is breaking the law.

In Honolulu, Hawaii, no person over the age of fourteen can legally wear a bathing suit on any street or highway unless covered by an outer garment reaching at least down to the knees.

It is unlawful for any female to appear in a bathing suit on a highway in Kentucky unless she is escorted by at least two officers or armed with a club.

In Payette, Idaho, any person without an occupation or business is subject to a fine.

Ice fishing is unlawful in Kansas.

Cab drivers are prohibited from smoking while driving a cab in Columbus, Ohio.

It is against the law to rob a bird's nest in a public cemetery in Oklahoma.

To adopt someone in Oklahoma, you must be at least ten years older than the person being adopted.

Throwing or placing a banana peel on the sidewalks within the city limits of Sherman, Texas, is unlawful.

It is against the law to put any hypnotized person in a display window in Harthshorne, Oklahoma.

In Oklahoma, it is the sheriff's duty to destroy prairie dogs in his county if the respective landowner refuses.

Any dog caught roaming around unleashed in Tuntutuliak Village, Alaska, will be shot after the second offense.

A California law makes it illegal to set up a mousetrap without a hunting license.

Accepting a gratuity or tip in Iowa is prohibited by the law.

In Winchester, Kentucky, it is against the law to carry water from any of the public fountains.

It is illegal to fall asleep in a bathtub in Detroit, Michigan.

In New York, it is unlawful for a man to greet another man on the street by placing the end of his thumb against the tip of his nose and wiggling his fingers at the same time.

No girl under the age of sixteen is allowed to sell newspapers or magazines on any street in any city of Oklahoma.

Bathing in any river or lake without wearing attire that covers from the neck to the knees is illegal in Portland, Oregon.

In Tuntutuliak Village, Alaska, any unmarried girl who gets pregnant is sent to the Bethel City jail with the man who got her pregnant until the baby is born.

Two people of the opposite sex cannot legally share a hotel room in Detroit unless they are husband and wife or parent and child.

The noise ordinances of Little Rock, Arkansas, prohibit dogs from barking after 6 p.m.

It is illegal in Little Rock, Arkansas, to try to pick up anyone of the opposite sex by whistling, coughing, winking, or staring at them along any of the streets or sidewalks.

If someone is convicted in Detroit of violating any state or federal law, the mayor can refuse a license to that person to serve soft drinks in his or her business.

It is prohibited by law to throw rice at weddings in Chillicothe, Ohio.

In Missouri, it is a misdemeanor to wear a hat or bonnet inside any licensed theater in the city during a performance.

It is illegal in Montana to wear a mask, false whiskers, or any other personal disguise for the purpose of evading discovery or identification if convicted of any public offense.

A woman may not legally take a bath in a business office in Carmel, California.

In Utah, a husband is responsible for every criminal act, except capital offenses, committed by his wife while he is in her presence.

A third party must be present for a physician or dentist to put a female patient to sleep with an anesthetic in West Virginia.

It is illegal to pawn the clothes off your back in New Hampshire.

Anyone guilty of using profanity in Oklahoma can be punished a dollar for each offense.

It is against the law to make an election bet of more than $5 in Virginia.

Driving a car while sleeping is against the law in Memphis, Tennessee.

In Nashville, Tennessee, it is considered a misdemeanor for any woman to work as a shoe shiner or barber in any establishment patronized by men.

Selling or giving away a toy pistol is a misdemeanor in Utah.

It is against the law in Roanoke, Virginia, for any woman to go to a saloon for the purpose of buying an intoxicating beverage or loitering.

In Virginia, a $100 fine is required if you are caught swearing at someone over the phone.

Throwing watermelon seeds on the sidewalk in Hammond, Indiana, is illegal.

It is against the law in Springfield, Illinois, for a boy to walk on a fence railing.

In Missouri, it is illegal to have a horse race, a cock fight, or games of any kind on Sunday.

It is just as illegal to pretend to be intoxicated as it is to actually be intoxicated in Iowa.

In Detroit, it is against the law to "display, expose for sale, or advertise for sale" any contraceptive or article for the prevention of venereal disease.

Eating or pretending to eat any snake, lizard, scorpion, etc., in public is illegal in Kansas.

It is against the law in Kansas to catch fish with your bare hands.

A male cannot legally wink at a female with whom he is unacquainted in the City of Ottumwa, Iowa.

In Georgia, a wife can legally divorce her husband if he is in the military service of the United States.

It is illegal to ride on a streetcar in Atlanta, Georgia, if a person has an offensive odor and the conductor requests him or her to leave.

In Sacramento, California, it is against the law for a building's doors to open inward instead of outward.

In California, it is unlawful for a goggle-fisherman to spearfish unless he is completely submerged underwater.

In Hartford, Connecticut, every theater owner in the city must bring good drinking water and sanitary cups for the free use of its customers at least once an hour.

Roosters are banned by law in Key West, Florida.

It is against the law for a man to make love to his wife with the smell of garlic, onions, or sardines on his breath in Alexandria, Minnesota. If a man's wife requests him to brush his teeth, the law mandates that he must obey.

A law in Bozeman, Montana, bans all sexual activity between members of the opposite sex in the front yard of a home after sundown if the couple is nude.

In Hastings, Nebraska, hotel owners are required to provide guests with clean and pressed nightshirts. The law was written to prevent couples, including those who are married, from sleeping together in the nude. The law requires them to wear the nightshirts even during sex.

In Norfolk, Virginia, a woman must wear a corset while in public. (Back in the days when the law was enforced, town corset inspector was a coveted civil-service job—for men only.)

The women of Merryville, Missouri, were prohibited from wearing corsets. Why? Because "the privilege of admiring the curvaceous, unencumbered body of a young woman should not be denied to the normal, red-blooded American male."

In Coeur d'Alene, Idaho, police officers are not permitted to walk up and knock on the window of a parked car. If an officer is suspicious that an act of sex is being performed, he or she must drive up from behind, honk his or her horn three times, and wait approximately two minutes before getting out to conduct an investigation.

In Carlsbad, New Mexico, couples are legally permitted to engage in sex while in a parked vehicle during their lunch break from work. They may do so as long as the car or van has drawn curtains to stop strangers from peeking in.

Helena, Montana, has a law that prohibits a woman from dancing on a table in a saloon or bar unless she has on at least three pounds, two ounces of clothing.

Women are not allowed to wear patent-leather shoes in Cleveland, Ohio. This law was passed to prevent a man from seeing a reflection of her underwear, that is, if she is wearing any.

It is not permitted for a woman to have sex with a man while riding in an ambulance within the boundaries of Tremonton, Utah. If arrested, she can be charged with a sexual misdemeanor and "her name is to be published in the local newspaper." The man, however, will not be charged, nor will his name be revealed.

Early Colonial Laws

In the first years of settlement in America, some of the harshest laws ever written were passed to keep the colonists in line.

For the most part, these laws were written to enforce religious devotion, a dominant factor in their lives. Here are some examples:

In 1618, it was decreed in Virginia that all who failed to attend church service would be imprisoned in the guardhouse, "lying ye night following and be a slave ye week following." Furthermore, Sunday dancing, fiddling, card playing, hunting, and fishing were forbidden.

In 1619, blue laws in Virginia were enacted that required men to dress according to their rank. Excess in dress was also discouraged by taxing one's wardrobe.

In 1634, Massachusetts passed a sumptuary law that prohibited the purchase of clothes that were woolen, linen, or silk with silver, gold, silk or thread lace on them. Slashed clothing was limited to a slash in each sleeve and in back.

In 1639, New England law censured men for wearing "immoderate great breeches," broad shoulder-bands, capes, and double ruffles.

In 1639, shopkeepers in New England who took more than a sixpence in shilling profit were accused of unfair trade and could be excommunicated.

In 1639, a woman of Plymouth convicted of adultery was sentenced to "be whipt at a cart tyle" and to "weare a badge upon her sleeve during her aboad." If found in public without the badge, she was to be "burned in the face with a hott iron." An adulteress's badge had the letters *AD* on it.

In 1639, a law in Massachusetts was passed against making a drinking toast. "The common custom of drinking to one another is a mere useless ceremony, and draweth on the abominable practice of drinking healths."

In 1646, a law in Massachusetts made it lawful to smoke tobacco only when on a journey five miles away from any town.

In 1647, in Connecticut, a blue law prohibited "social" smoking. It was permissible to use tobacco once a day, at meals or elsewhere "and then not in the company of any other." Tobacco could, however, be used in the confines of one's home.

In 1647, a Massachusetts law prohibited any Jesuit Roman Catholic priest from entering territory under Puritan jurisdiction. Any suspected person who could not clear himself was to be banished; a second offense carried a death penalty.

Frivolous Laws in the Making

So many of the silly laws on the books are vestiges of olden times, it's heartening to see that our current crop of lawmakers is determined not to be left out. The Associated Press recently reported on these new bills: exempting armless motorists from paying tolls on the New Jersey Turnpike; legalizing rubber-duck races in Nebraska; shielding real estate agents against suits for failure to inform buyers that someone had died in a house; and outlawing tripping a horse on purpose. State legislators are also infamous for piling on the official birds, beasts, and other miscellany. Now Pennsylvania and Indiana want state tartans like the Scottish clans.

Chapter 2

HOW MANY LAWYERS ARE THERE? AND OTHER LEGAL TRIVIA

In this chapter, you'll find hundreds of interesting facts about the law and those who practice it. Even if you're not in the legal profession, you'll discover dozens of bits of information about attorneys and the law that even they don't know.

More Than Our Share

The United States has 5 percent of the world's population and 70 percent of its lawyers.

Source: *Business Insurance*, January 27, 1992, page 29.

Passing the Bar

About 75 percent of the people who take the bar examination in the United States get a passing grade. In contrast, only 2 percent pass the bar examination in Japan.

Source: *New Jersey Law Journal*, June 22, 1992, page 15.

The O.J. Simpson Case

The Los Angeles Central Criminal Division disposed of 474 felony preliminary hearings in the time it took to dispose of the O.J. Simpson preliminary hearing.

Source: *USA Today*, July 12, 1994, page A-1

The Tort Cost

The "tort tax" allegedly accounts for about 30 percent of the price of a stepladder and 95 percent of the price of childhood vaccines. A tort tax is a premium added to the price of a product as a result of damages assessed against the maker of such product in a product liability lawsuit.

Source: Rubenstein, Ed, "Punitive Damages," *National Review*, November 4, 1991.

O.J. Simpson Defense

Outside lawyers and experts estimated that O.J. Simpson's legal costs exceeded $5 million for his trial. These estimates were compiled assuming seven lawyers charging $51,000 per day, a forensics expert for $5,000 per day, four DNA experts at $6,000 per day as well as a toll free number and additional investigation expenses. One 18 hour work day for seven lawyers charging between $400 and $650 per hour is at least $51,000. Before joining the defense team, Los Angeles lawyer Johnnie Cochran, Jr., set a conservative total of about $2 million. Simpson's lead lawyer, Robert Shapiro, reportedly charges a top hourly rate of $650 per hour. If he bills 18 hours a day, seven days a week, his bill would be $350,000 per month. However, most lawyers and experts believe that Shapiro agreed to a total fee of around $1 million. Other celebrities have paid millions of dollars for their defense. Mike Tyson reportedly spent $2 million to defend himself unsuccessfully on rape charges in Indianapolis. William Kennedy Smith spent as much as $2 million, his entire trust fund, to win an acquittal at his rape trial in Palm Beach, Florida. The Menendez Brothers, accused of murdering their parents, spent more than $1.5 million in their separate Los Angeles murder trials, which ended with hung juries.

The California County handling the Simpson case had virtually unlimited resources. The county employs 1,800 deputies, a county coroner's staff of 145, and 7,785 police officers.

Records from Mr. Simpson's divorce in 1992 put his wealth at $10.8 million. Half of that was the assessed

Ratio of Scientists and Engineers to Lawyers

Country	Ratio
Japan	115.5
United Kingdom	14.5
Germany	9.1
United States	4.8

Source: Rubenstein, Ed, "Punitive Damages," *National Review,* November 4, 1991.

Too Many Lawyers . . .

Country	Lawyers per 100,000 Population
United States	307.4
Britain	102.7
Germany	82
Japan	12.1

Source: Ibid.

... And Multiplying

Year	Number
1971	355,242
1980	542,205
1990	750,000
1992	825,000
2000	1,000,000 *

*estimate

Source: American Bar Association; National Center for State Courts; *Business Week*; *Business Insurance*, January 27, 1992, page 29.

Too Many Lawyers in the United States?

More and more Americans think the United States has too many lawyers.

Response	1986	1993
Too few	9%	5%
Right number	21	13
Too many	55	73

Source: Penn & Schoen national poll for *The National Law Journal,* August 10, 1992.

Number of Lawsuits in the United States

Year	State Court Filings (in Millions)
1984	14.1
1986	15.5
1988	16.6
1990	18.4

Source: Ibid.

World's Largest Law Firm

In 1992, Baker & McKenzie, employing 1,604, was the world's largest law firm. The firm has 470 partners, and billings for fiscal year 1992 were $503.5 million. The firm was founded in Chicago in 1949.

Source: *The American Lawyer,* June 1993.

Average Profits per Partner for Top 100 Law Firms in the United States

In 1992, the average partner profits for the nation's 100 largest law firms were $406,000, well below the 1980 figure of $433,000—the highest average profits per partner since *The American Lawyer* began its annual survey.

Source: Ibid.

Peak Year for Firm with Largest Gross Revenue

In 1989, Skadden Arps, the huge New York law firm, had record revenues of about $517.5 million, and the average partner share was almost $1.2 million. The firm's 1992 revenues were $440 million and profits per partner were $885,000.

Source: Caplan, Lincoln, *Skadden: Power, Money and the Rise of a Legal Empire*, Farrar, Straus & Giroux: New York, 1993; *The American Lawyer.*

Legal Malpractice

Lawyers are beginning to get a taste of their own medicine. As Richard Perez-Pena reports for *The New York Times,* legal malpractice suits are a growth industry. The lawyers in Perez-Pena's article speculated that with the breakdown of community, the personal lawyer/golf-buddy is going the way of the family doctor. No statistics were available, but the closest documentation is the rise in insurance premiums, from little to no charge by insurers to the current $15,000 a year. The turncoats who dare to attack their own kind are pariahs. As one legal malpractice specialist put it, "The lawyers we sue all take it very personally; they're angry and nasty. Other lawyers think we're scum; even judges look on us disfavorably." In their defense, another legal malpractice lawyer retorts, "There are idiots out there practicing law." When the sharks go after each other, it's certain the scales will fly.

First African American Supreme Court Judge

Thurgood Marshall became the first African American to serve on the United States Supreme Court when President Lyndon B. Johnson appointed him on June 13, 1967. Marshall retired from the court on June 27, 1991, and was replaced by Clarence Thomas. — *the second Af. Amer. to serve* '

Largest Divorce Settlement

The reported settlement achieved in 1982 by the lawyers of Soraya Khashoggi was $950 million plus property from her husband Adnan.

Source: *Guinness Book of Records*, New York: Sterling Publishing Co., 1992.

Largest Inadequate Divorce Offer

Mrs. Anne Bass, former wife of Sid Bass of Texas, was reported to have rejected $535 million as inadequate to live in the style to which she had been made accustomed.

Source: Ibid. 1992.

The United States Divorce Rate

The United States has the highest divorce rate in the world, double that of England and more than 10 times that of Japan. In 1960, 9.2 out of every 1,000 marriages in the United States broke up, and by 1988 over 20 of every 1,000 marriages in the United States ended. Nearly 1.2 million American couples divorced in 1990, with about half of those involving children under the age of 18.

Source: *The Atlanta Journal and Constitution,* November 29, 1993, Section A, page 9.

States with Highest Divorce Rates

The following is a list of states with the highest divorce rates:

Ranks	State	Divorces per 1,000 Population
1	Nevada	14.1
2	Arizona	7.1
3	Oklahoma	7.1
4	Arkansas	7.0
5	Alaska	6.9
6	Wyoming	6.9
7	Tennessee	6.5
8	Florida	6.3
9	Kansas	6.2
10	Idaho	6.0

Source: United States National Center for Health Statistics (1991).

First Legal Society in America

The New York Bar Association was organized by lawyers of New York City to defend themselves against attacks by Lt. Governor Cadwallader Colden. In 1765, the group spearheaded colonial resistance to the Stamp Act.

Source: Carruth, Gorton, *The Encyclopedia of American Facts and Dates*, 8th ed., New York: Harper & Row Publishers, 1987.

First Legal Journal in the United States

In 1808, the American Law Journal was published in Baltimore by John Elihu Hall, professor of rhetoric at the University of Maryland. Hall's publication is believed to be the first legal journal in American history. It was terminated in 1817.

Source: Ibid.

First College Law Instruction in the United States

The first law course offered in the United States was by King's College (now Columbia University), New York City, in 1755.

Source: Kane, Joseph, *Famous First Facts*, New York: The H.W. Wilson Company, 1981.

First Woman in United States to Practice Law

Arabella A. Mansfield of Mount Pleasant, Iowa, who was admitted to practice law in June 1869, had studied in a law office and at home. Section 1610 of the Iowa Code of 1851 had until then prevented women from being admitted to the bar by a statute providing admission to "any white male person . . ."

Source: Ibid.

First Black Woman to Get Law Degree

Charlotte E. Ray was the first black woman in the United States to receive a law degree. She finished her studies at Howard University in 1872.

Source: Ibid.

First Black Woman Judge

The first black woman judge was the Honorable Jane M. Bolin of New York, who was appointed judge in the Domestic Relations Court in New York in 1939. Not only was she the first black woman judge, she was also the first black woman to graduate from Yale Law School and to be admitted to the Bar Association of the City of New York.

Source: Ibid.

The Death Sentence

There were 2,575 prisoners sentenced to death as of December 31, 1992. All of these prisoners had been convicted of murder. Texas had the most prisoners sentenced to death at that time: 344.

Source: U.S. Department of Justice, Bureau of Justice Statistics Bulletin, Capital Punishment 1992.

First State to Abolish Capital Punishment

Michigan became the first state to abolish capital punishment in 1847.

Source: *The 1991 Information Please Almanac*, Boston: Houghton Mifflin Co., 1991.

Death Row

Since the United States Supreme Court reinstated capital punishment in 1976, a total of 3,979 persons entered state prisons under sentences of death; 1,598 persons had their death sentences removed as the result of court action, commutations, or death while under sentence; 188 persons were executed. The following table details the executions between 1977 and 1992:

Means of Execution	White	Black	Hispanic	Native American	Asian
Lethal Injection	47	23	11	1	0
Electrocution	50	47	1	0	0
Lethal Gas	4	3	0	0	0
Firing Squad	1	0	0	0	0
Total	102	73	12	1	0

Source: U.S. Department of Justice, Bureau of Justice Statistics Bulletin, Capital Punishment 1992.

Classified Information at the United States Patent Office

The United States Patent and Trademark office has 385 classifications and 100,000 subclassifications of things that are patentable.

Source: Foster, Frank, and Robert L. Shook, *Patents, Copyrights & Trademarks*, New York: John Wiley & Sons, 1989.

Capital Punishment

As of December 1992, the following states had a death penalty for different capital offenses:

State	Minimum Age	Method of Execution
Alabama	16	Electrocution
Arizona	None	Lethal gas
Arkansas	14	Lethal injection or electrocution (a)
California	18	Lethal gas
Colorado	18	Lethal injection or lethal gas (b)
Connecticut	18	Electrocution
Delaware	None	Lethal injection
Florida	None	Electrocution
Georgia	17	Electrocution
Idaho	None	Lethal injection or firing squad
Illinois	17	Lethal injection
Indiana	16	Electrocution
Kentucky	16	Electrocution
Louisiana	16	Electrocution
Maryland	16	Electrocution

(a) Arkansas authorizes lethal injection for those whose capital offense occurred after July 4, 1983; for those whose offense occurred before that date, the condemned prisoner may select lethal injection or electrocution.

(b) Colorado authorizes lethal gas for those whose crimes occurred before July 1, 1988, and lethal injection for those whose crimes occurred on or after July 1, 1988.

State	Minimum Age	Method of Execution
Mississippi	16 (c)	Lethal injection (d)
Missouri	16	Lethal injection or lethal gas
Montana	None	Lethal injection or hanging
Nebraska	18	Electrocution
Nevada	16	Lethal injection
New Hampshire	17	Lethal injection or hanging (e)
New Jersey	18	Lethal injection
New Mexico	18	Lethal injection
North Carolina	17 (f)	Lethal injection or lethal gas
Ohio	18	Electrocution
Oklahoma	16	Lethal injection
Oregon	18	Lethal injection
Pennsylvania	None	Lethal injection
South Carolina	None	Electrocution
South Dakota	10 (g)	Lethal injection
Tennessee	18	Electrocution
Texas	17	Lethal injection
Utah	14	Lethal injection or firing squad
Virginia	15	Electrocution
Wyoming	16	Lethal injection

(c) The Mississippi statute defines the minimum age as 13, but the effective age is 16 based on an interpretation of United States Supreme Court decisions by the Mississippi attorney general's office.

(d) Mississippi authorizes lethal injection for those convicted after July 1, 1984; lethal gas is used to execute those convicted prior to that date.

(e) New Hampshire authorizes hanging only if lethal injection cannot be given.

(f) Age required is 17 unless the murderer was incarcerated for murder when a subsequent murder occurred, then the age may be 14.

(g) The age is 10 only after a transfer hearing to try a juvenile as an adult.

Source: *The Book of the States,* Vol. 30 (The Counsel of State Governments, 1994–95 Edition)

Execution in the United States

The United States had 31 executions in 1992—the highest number since the death penalty was reinstated in 1976. The prisoners executed in 1992 had been under a sentence of death an average of 9 years and 6 months. The following is the number of state executions since 1976:

State	Number of Executions
Texas	54
Florida	29
Louisiana	20
Virginia	17
Georgia	15
Alabama	10
Missouri	7
Nevada	5
North Carolina	5
Arkansas	4
Mississippi	4
South Carolina	4
Utah	4
Oklahoma	3
Indiana	2
Arizona	1
California	1
Delaware	1
Illinois	1
Wyoming	1

Source: U.S. Department of Justice, Bureau of Justice Statistics Bulletin, Capital Punishment 1992; NAACP Legal Defense and Educational Fund.

Too Much Litigation

In 1989, approximately 18 million new civil cases were filed in the United States' federal and state courts. That's about one for every ten adults. In the federal courts, the number of lawsuits filed each year has almost tripled in the past thirty years—from approximately 90,000 in 1960 to more than 250,000 in 1990. The annual cost for litigation to American society is an estimated $300 billion. No wonder an estimated 70 percent of the world's lawyers live in America.

Source: President's Council on Competitiveness (1991).

An Abundance of Lawyers

In Washington, D.C., one lawyer exists for every 17 people! In contrast, North Carolina has the fewest per capita with only one lawyer for every 704 residents.

Source: *U.S. News & World Report*, February 13, 1989, Vol. 106, No. 6, page 84.

The First United States Patent

On April 10, 1790, a patent bill was passed by both houses of Congress. President Washington signed the first patent act. A separate copyright act was enacted on May 31, 1790. When the first patent was issued that year, George Washington and Thomas Jefferson actually signed it.

Source: Foster, Frank, and Robert L. Shook, *Patents, Copyrights & Trademarks,* New York: John Wiley & Sons, 1989.

Average Patent Search

The average patent search takes about 15 hours.

Source: Ibid.

Getting a Patent

The average patent pendency time in 1988 was 19.9 months. Of the 148,183 patent applications that year, 83,594 were issued. About 45 percent of the applications were from foreign residents, and about 47 percent of them were issued.

Source: United States Department of Commerce, Patent and Trademark Office.

Longest Lease

The longest lease on record is 10 million years for a plot for a sewage tank adjoining Columb Barracks, Ireland, signed on December 3, 1888.

Source: *Guinness Book of World Records*, New York: Sterling Publishing Co., 1990.

First Income Tax

Federal income tax was levied in the United States in 1913. It called for 1 percent of income above $3,000 for singles; and above $4,000 for married couples. A 1 percent surtax on incomes above $20,000 graduated to 6 percent for those individuals with earnings above $500,000.

Source: Wallechinsky, David, and Irving Wallace, *The People's Almanac #2*, New York: Bantam Books, 1978.

I'm Guilty, Your Honor

The average sentence varies according to how you plead. As the following data indicates, a guilty plea gets a lighter sentence.

Offense	Trial by Jury	Trial by Judge	Guilty Plea
Murder	28 years	21 years	14 years
Robbery	24 years	15 years	10 years
Rape	18 years	14 years	11 years
Aggravated assault	14 years	9 years	7 years
Burglary	10 years	5 years	6 years
Drug trafficking	8 years	10 years	10 years
Larceny	4 years	4 years	4 years

Source: United States Department of Justice

Unknown Motives

Of American murders, 23 percent have an unknown motive.

Source: *Statistical Abstract of the United States*, 1987; Bureau of the Census; United States Department of Commerce.

Overcrowded Prisons

Although prison capacity increased 60 percent between 1984 and 1990, the number of prisoners over this period increased nearly 70 percent, resulting in prisons holding 122 percent of intended capacity. In 1990, there were 957 prisons—with a designed total capacity of 541,500—holding 658,800 prisoners.

Source: American Bar Association, The State of Criminal Justice (1993).

Jury Duty

Forty-five percent of adult Americans have been called for jury duty, and 17 percent of adult Americans have served through an actual trial, according to a 1991 survey.

Source: *Michigan Lawyers Weekly*, June 24, 1991.

Paid Leave for Jury Duty

Ninety-one percent of American employees of medium and large firms get paid leave for jury duty.

Source: *BNA Pension & Benefits Reporter*, Vol. 16, No. 50,
December 11, 1989, page 2093.

The Fear of Jury Duty

For Americans, serving jury duty has always been a dreaded chore. There is plenty of history behind this fear. In colonial days, jurors were locked in a small room with no ventilation and were denied food and water in an attempt to inspire a quick verdict. If the jurors returned with the wrong decisions, they too were charged with a crime. As more and more laws were passed, the rules of evidence expanded and trials became longer, which resulted in more technical and increasingly boring hours for jurors. Trial lawyers have tried to change the boredom by replacing endless hours of testimony with computer animation, video reconstructions, color charts and graphics to better explain the evidence.

Each year, over 5 million Americans are summoned for jury duty to render verdicts in approximately 120,000 trials. Prospective jurors are chosen at random from voter registration lists. Jurors are paid per day of service and some states also pay jurors for traveling. When people report for jury duty, they are often shown a video tape explaining the jury system. The jury selection process begins with voir dire, which simply means "to speak the truth." Prospective jurors are questioned concerning possible relationships they may have with the parties involved or about whether they have any prior knowledge pertaining to the facts of the case. The judge and the attorneys ask the jurors specific questions to determine if the jurors can be totally impartial. Each side has a determined number of "peremptory challenges" (for which no reason must be given) and "challenges for cause" (for which they must state the cause to the judge, who will then rule whether the attorney's challenge is proper). If a prospective juror is chosen to serve on a jury for a trial, the jurors are prohibited from speaking to any person about anything that occurs in the courtroom. Jurors are prohibited from conducting their own investigation of the case, visiting the scene of the accident or alleged crime, or making any attempt to question witnesses.

The judicial system depends on juries. The United States Constitution guarantees its citizens the right to a trial by jury of our peers. When summoned for jury duty, Americans should look upon it as an opportunity to serve their country, their community, and their fellow citizens.

Source: *The Atlanta Journal and Constitution*, June 14, 1992, Section D, page 1; *St. Petersburg Times*, May 2, 1992, page 2.

The Make-Up of Jurors

According to the National Center for State Courts, the average juror is a white, married, college-educated woman between 30 and 49 years old. The following is a glance at jurors in two state courts:

State	Male	Female	White	Registered Voter
Boston, MA	46%	54%	95%	93%
Denver, CO	40%	60%	77%	89%

Source: National Center for State Courts.

Average Length of Jury Deliberations

The average length of time that juries spend deliberating to reach a verdict in criminal trials is as follows:

Crime	Time
Homicide	5 hr. 30 min.
Rape	3 hr. 40 min.
Aggravated assault	2 hr. 38 min.
Burglary	2 hr. 19 min.
Narcotics	2 hr. 12 min.
Robbery	1 hr. 50 min.
Theft	1 hr. 40 min.

Source: National Center for State Courts (based on comparative study of nine courts in New Jersey, Colorado, and California).

Killings by Handguns

The number of people killed by handguns for the 1988–1989 period was as follows:

Country	Total	People per Million
United States	9,602	38.3
Switzerland	53	7.9
Israel	25	5.7
Sweden	19	2.3
Australia	13	0.8
Japan	46	0.4
Canada	8	0.3
United Kingdom	7	0.1

Source: Handgun Control, Inc.; *Uniform Reports 1990*, Washington, D.C., 1991, page 12; Text-Handgun Control Inc.; Death Penalty Information Center.

Minorities Arrested

While minorities account for fewer than one-third of all arrests, minorities accounted for over half of the jail inmates, prisoners, probationers, and parolees in 1990. In addition, over three-fifths of juveniles placed in custody were minorities.

Source: American Bar Association, *The State of Criminal Justice* (1993).

Soaring Crime Rates in Small Cities

From 1985 to 1990, the murder rate in many of America's cities with populations under 1 million soared. The following table shows which cities had the greatest increases in crime.

City	Percent Increase in Murders 1985–1990
Milwaukee	126
New Orleans	101
Jacksonville	84
Memphis	71
Charlotte	60
Baltimore	43
Kansas City, MO	38
Cleveland	23

Source: City police departments.

Case Filings

Over 100,000,000 cases were filed in state trial courts in 1990, of which 13 percent were criminal cases, 18 percent were civil cases, 2 percent were juvenile cases, and 67 percent were traffic cases.

Source: American Bar Association, *The State of Criminal Justice* (1993).

Employees For Justice

In 1990, the justice system employed over 1.6 million full-time employees. Almost half were for police protection and nearly one-third were for correctional services. Only 1 percent were for public defender services.

Source: Ibid.

Product Defects

In a five-year period from 1987 to 1992, the likelihood of winning a product liability lawsuit—a lawsuit against a manufacturer due to damages resulting from a defective product—dropped from 54 percent to 41 percent.

Source: *Wall Street Journal,* July 12, 1994, page B-3.

Releasing Criminals

According to a 1990 study by the United States Department of Justice, an estimated 65 percent of defendants who had felony charges filed against them were released prior to the disposition of their case. Approximately 25 percent had a bench warrant issued for their arrest because they did not appear in court as scheduled, and 8 percent of the released defendants were still fugitives after one year.

Source: United States Department of Justice, Bureau of Justice
Statistics Bulletin, Pretrial Release of Felony Defendants, 1990.

Legislator Pay

Of all states, New York's legislators earn the highest salary—$57,500 per year, while New Hampshire's legislators earn the lowest salary—$100 per year.

Source: Ibid.

Crowded Cells

At the end of 1992, state and federal prisons in nearly three-quarters of the states were operating over maximum capacity. The ten states with the most severe crowding are listed in the following table:

State	Percent Over
California	91
Ohio	77
Nebraska	50
Pennsylvania	49
Vermont	47
Massachusetts	44
Michigan	44
Virginia	39
Wisconsin	39
Iowa	38

1994 state figures for Ohio have increased to 84.7 percent.

Source: United States Department of Justice, Bureau of Justice Statistics Bulletin, May 1993.

Time in the Slammer

The average time spent incarcerated is four years, ten months; the median sentence is about three years. State prisons have an average stay of six years, nine months, whereas local jails have an average stay of nine months.

Source: National Judicial Reporting Program of the United States Department of Justice.

Guilty but Not Imprisoned

Of American murderers convicted in the United States District Court, 30 percent are not imprisoned.

Source: *Statistical Abstract of the United States,* 1987.

Sentencing by State Courts

State courts send about 46 percent of convicted felons to state prisons, 21 percent to local jails, 31 percent to straight pro- bation, and 2 percent receive other nonincarceration sentences.

Source: National Judicial Reporting Program of the United States Department of Justice.

Murder and Non-Negligent Manslaughter in the United States

In 1988, 20,675 people were killed by other people in the United States, or about 8.4 murders per 100,000 inhabitants.

Source: United States Department of Justice; Federal Bureau of Investigation.

Violent Crime in the United States

In 1989, a total of 4.9 percent of households experienced a violent crime, with 3.8 percent suffering assault, 1 percent rob- bery, and 0.1 percent rape. This figure was up from 4.8 percent in 1988.

Source: United States Department of Justice.

Escapees from Prison

In 1988, some 10,351 convicts escaped from United States prisons, and only 76 percent were recaptured.

Source: United States Department of Justice.

The Legal Meter Runs and Runs

In 1977, the City of New York passed a law requiring window guards for apartments with children under age ten. This prompted a vote by the co-op board at 360 W. 36th Street ruling that the cost for such equipment must be paid for by the residents who need it rather than spreading the cost around equally. Alec and Suzi Diacou, whose third child was only a month old at the time, refused to pay the $909 charged for the iron bars installed across 32 windows of their ninth-floor unit.

The co-op board brought suit against the Diacous. After all, it was a matter of principle. If the Diacous did not pay, it would set an expensive precedent that other residents might follow. The co-op hired the law firm, Gallet Dreyer & Berkey, and by October 1987, three hours and twenty-five minutes of legal work were applied to settlement efforts and other communications with the defendants. The co-op's bill came to $315. When a settlement couldn't be reached, more legal work was required, and by June 1988, the tab totaled $1,015, more than the cost of the window guards.

On a matter of principle, the co-op board decided to go all out to win. By November 1988, its legal fees totaled $5,504. By January, after drafting, editing, and serving documents, another $3,996 was added to the bill. By this point, the co-op's legal expenses were more than nine times the cost of what was at stake! On January 26, a New York Civil Court ruled that "logic and substantial justice as well as lease provision" required the Diacous to pay the $909. The Diacous appealed, and the legal expenses continued to climb. The first appeals court ruled that the cost of $909 must be shared by both parties. The co-op board elected to take the case to the next appellate level. At issue now was who would pay the legal fees.

A provision under the ownership contract stated that when a dispute occurs between the co-op and a unit's owner, the loser must reimburse the winner's legal fees. For obvious reasons, both parties had an added incentive to win the case.

The litigation went on and on, up to the New York State Supreme Court. When it was all over, the co-op board had legal expenses totaling a whopping $73,000! The Diacous paid $30,000 to their attorneys and were ordered by the court to pay $30,000 of the co-op's legal fees. The case was a costly lesson for both parties. In retrospect, Mr. Diacou says, "I'm a man converted." He advises: "Anything you can possibly do to avoid a lawsuit, do it."

Source: Lambert, Wade, "Ever Hear the One About the Lawyers and Window Bars?," *Wall Street Journal*, March 23, 1994, page 1.

Few Death Sentences for Murder

About 2 percent of those convicted of murder were sentenced to death in 1992.

Source: United States Department of Justice, Bureau of Justice Statistics Bulletin, Capital Punishment 1992.

Women Prisoners

In 1993, 29,000 women spent time in jail. Of them, 80 percent were mothers, most of them unmarried.

Source: *Chicago Sun Times*, April 30, 1994, page 20.

Nighttime Crime

Of American robberies, 54 percent are committed during the night.

Source: United States Department of Justice, Bureau of Justice Statistics, Criminal Victimization in the United States, 1992.

White Collar Crime

When people are tried for a white collar crime, nearly 75 percent are convicted, but studies suggest that only about 15 percent of such crimes are ever detected.

Source: The United Way.

DNA Fingerprinting

The odds of two people having the same DNA, other than identical twins, is 30 billion to 1.

Source: *Columbus Dispatch*, June 18, 1989.

What an Ex-Wife Gets

Length of Marriage (Years)	Percent of Assets
5 or less	0–25
5–10	15–36
10 or more	33–45

Source: Raoul Felder, American Bar Association.

Picking a Jury—It's in the Stars

The reason a jury has twelve members goes back to ancient days when court astrologers did the picking. They made their selection according to the juror's sign. This was done in fairness to the defendant on the theory that the twelve jurors would be of every possible type of personality.

Getting Your Share of Lawsuits

The average American during his or her lifetime will be involved in five major legal battles. If you're average, these will involve buyer versus seller, tenant versus landlord, driver versus driver, husband versus wife, and insured versus insurance company.

Starting Salaries of Associate Lawyers in 19 United States Cities

City	High (1990)	Low (1990)	Median (1990)	Median (1989)
New York	$86,000	$65,000	$83,000	$82,000
Chicago	73,000	52,500	70,000	68,500
Los Angeles	75,000	65,000	70,000	65,000
Washington, D.C.	75,000	63,000	70,000	66,000
Boston	69,000	60,000	66,000	66,000
San Francisco	70,000	60,000	65,000	65,000
Cleveland	70,000	59,000	64,000	64,000
Houston	64,000	51,000	61,000	61,000
Philadelphia	63,000	40,000	61,000	62,000
Atlanta	60,000	58,000	60,000	58,000
Dallas	62,500	47,000	60,000	59,000
Detroit	65,000	55,000	58,000	52,000
Phoenix	60,000	52,000	56,250	52,000
Minneapolis/ St. Paul	58,000	42,000	54,500	49,000
St. Louis	56,000	40,000	53,000	50,000
Baltimore	60,000	52,000	52,500	51,000
Kansas City	52,000	48,500	50,000	49,250
New Orleans	51,000	48,000	50,000	45,000
Seattle	52,000	46,000	50,000	N.A.

Source: *Of Counsel*, Vol. 10, No. 9, May 6, 1991.

How Much They Earn

The following is the average total compensation for U.S. law firm partners by specialty:

Intellectual property	$245,607
Commercial real estate	211,656
Environmental	189,166
Litigation	187,748
Taxes	186,631
Labor	178,899
Insurance defense	165,851
Bankruptcy	164,315
Probate and estates	155,776
Family law	140,329

Source: Altman Weil Pensa Publications, Inc. 1994 *Survey of Law Firm Economics.*

More and More Women Entering Law School

In 1967, 4.5 percent of those entering law school were women. In 1993, women accounted for 43 percent.

Source: American Bar Association.

Few Women in Law Enforcement

Only 11 percent or 1,141 of the 11,000 special agents in 1991 were women. And in 1990, only 1.4 percent of high-ranking police supervisors were women.

Source: *National Law Journal;* The American Bar Foundation; The Police Foundation, federal government spokesman.

Top 30 Largest Corporate Legal Shops in the United States

Rank	Company	Number of Attorneys 1990–1991	1989–1990
1	Exxon	342	322
2	General Electric	331	330
3	IBM	331	351
4	AT&T	308	304
5	Prudential	305	301
6	Citicorp	283	290
7	Sears	276	282
8	Chevron	269	269
9	American Express	194	196
10	Amoco	174	160
11	Ford	165	167
12	Du Pont	160	224
13	United Technologies	154	139
14	Mobil	151	144
15	Aetna	144	131
16	BellSouth	140	136
17	General Motors	140	141
18	ITT	139	146
19	NYNEX	138	144
20	Metropolitan Life	135	121
21	Shell	131	129
22	Westinghouse	128	117
23	Chase Manhattan	127	122
24	Texaco	123	112
25	U.S. West	121	122

Rank	Company	Number of Attorneys	
		1990–1991	**1989–1990**
26	BankAmerica	109	111
26	Southwestern Bell	109	116
28	Bell Atlantic	108	97
28	Time Warner	108	63
30	ARCO	107	98

Source: *Of Counsel*, Vol. 10, No. 12, June 17, 1991.

Back-to-Work-Mother Lawyers

Of women lawyers on maternity leave, 95 percent are back to work within a year.

Source: American Bar Association.

Male Lawyers Make More

In the early 1990s, 6 percent of male lawyers and 15 percent of women lawyers made under $25,000 a year. At the same time, 27 percent of men and only 9 percent of woman made $100,000 or more a year.

Source: American Bar Association.

Million Dollar Verdicts

In 1962, only one verdict was given for a million dollars or more. In 1990 alone, 703 verdicts awarded over a million dollars, making a total of 5,032 million-dollar verdicts since 1962.

Source: *The Lawyers Almanac 1992*, Englewood Cliffs, NJ: Prentice Hall, 1992.

Top 25 Law Schools in the United States

Rank School	Overall score	Reputation rank by academics	Reputation rank by lawyers & judges	Average median '93 LSAT score	1993 median starting salary
1 Yale University	100.0	1	2	45	$66,059
2 Harvard University	93.5	1	1	44	67,193
3 University of Chicago	90.6	1	7	45	71,000
4 Stanford University	90.4	1	3	44	65,000
5 Columbia University	85.5	5	6	43	78,325
6 University of Michigan	84.0	5	4	44	59,604
7 New York University	83.9	8	11	45	76,688
8 University of Virginia	81.4	8	5	42	63,000
9 Duke University	81.2	11	9	44	60,172
10 University of Pennsylvania	79.1	8	10	42	64,600
11 Georgetown University	77.8	15	8	43	66,000
12 University of California at Berkeley	76.7	5	12	44	58,000
13 Cornell University	76.0	11	15	43	66,250
14 Northwestern University	75.2	11	13	41	65,075
15 University of Texas at Austin	71.6	11	14	41	52,567
16 University of Southern California	68.0	17	34	43	66,720
17 Vanderbilt University	67.6	19	16	41	55,000
18 University of California at Los Angeles	67.3	15	17	42	62,670
19 University of Iowa	62.4	19	31	39	50,000
20 University of California at Hastings	61.6	23	18	42	62,742
21 University of Wisconsin	60.2	19	27	40	47,500

Rank School	Overall score	Reputation rank by academics	Reputation rank by lawyers & judges	Average median '93 LSAT score	1993 median starting salary
22 George Washington University	59.6	25	20	40	61,000
23 University of Minnesota at Twin Cities	59.6	17	22	41	45,665
24 Notre Dame	59.1	40	19	41	56,885
25 University of North Carolina at Chapel Hill	59.1	19	23	41	40,500

Source: *U.S. News & World Report*; College Research Group; the colleges; Market Facts Inc., March 21, 1994, page 72.

First Woman Law School Graduate

Ada H. Kepley was the first woman to graduate from law school. She graduated from Union College of Law in Chicago, Illinois, on June 30, 1870.

Source: Kane, Joseph, *Famous First Facts*, New York: H.W. Wilson Company, 1991.

Lawyers in the White House

Of the first 42 United States presidents, 26 were lawyers.

Source: Attridge, James O'Neil, "A Lawyer in the White House," *The California Lawyer Magazine,* September 1988.

Tuitions of the Top 25 United States Law Schools

The following are 1990 out-of-state yearly tuition fees of the 25 top law schools in the United States.

Rank	School	Tuition
1	Yale University	$15,435
2	Harvard University	14,475
3	University of Chicago	15,720
4	Stanford University	14,894
5	Columbia University	16,070
6	University of Michigan	15,748
7	New York University	16,600
8	University of Virginia	10,110
9	Duke University	15,300
10	University of Pennsylvania	15,066
11	Georgetown University	15,430
12	University of California at Berkeley	8,830
13	Cornell University	15,900
14	Northwestern University	15,532
15	University of Texas at Austin	6,010
16	University of Southern California	16,380
17	Vanderbilt University	14,750
18	University California at Los Angeles	9,035
19	University of Iowa	7,698
20	University of California at Hastings	8,664
21	University of Wisconsin at Madison	9,123
22	George Washington University	15,250
23	University of Minnesota at Twin Cities	8,730
24	University of Notre Dame	12,980
25	University of North Carolina at Chapel Hill	7,013

Source: *U.S. News & World Report*; College Research Group; the colleges; Market Facts Inc., March 21, 1994, page 72.

Famous People Who Were Once Lawyers

Person	Occupation
Mel Allen	Sports announcer
Charles Brackett	Producer/screenwriter
Rossano Brazzi	Actor
Michael Cacoyannis	Movie director
Hoagy Carmichael	Songwriter
John Cleese	Comic actor
Howard Cosell	Sports commentator
John van Druten	Playwright
Erle Stanley Gardner	Author
Romain Gary	Author
John Grisham	Author
Julio Iglesias	Singer
Meir Kahane	Rabbi, Jewish Defense League founder
Tony LaRussa	Major League baseball manager
Leo McCarey	Movie director
Ozzie Nelson	Actor
James Pike	Clergyman
Otto Preminger	Movie director
Quentin Reynolds	Author
Geraldo Rivera	TV personality
Murray Schisgal	Playwright
Scott Turow	Author

Source: Lucaire, Ed, *The Celebrity Almanac,* New York: Prentice Hall, 1991, page 117.

Lax Marijuana Laws

The following lists the ten states with the softest marijuana statutes:

Rank	State	Law
1	Alaska	Legal for personal use in home; personal use not in home: $0–100
2	Ohio	Possession of up to 100 grams: $0–100
3	Oregon	Possession of up to 1 ounce: $0–100; over 1 ounce: 0–10 years and $2,500
4	California	Possession of up to 1 ounce: $0–100; over 1 ounce: 0–6 months and $500
5	Minnesota	Up to 1 ounce not in vehicle: $0–100
6	Maine	Possession of up to 1.5 ounce: $0–200
7	Colorado	Possession of up to 1 ounce in private: $0–100; in public: 0–15 days and $100
8	Nebraska	Possession of up to 1 ounce: $100 and drug education
9	New Mexico	Possession of up to 1 ounce: 0–15 days and $100
10	South Dakota	Possession of up to 1 ounce: 0–30 days and $100; over 1 ounce: 0–1 year and $1,000

Source: National Organization for the Reform of Marijuana Laws.

The Harsh Penalties of LSD

The following table compares the prescribed prison sentence for a first-time offender with $1,500 worth of LSD against sentences for other federal crimes.

Crime	Minimum	Maximum
LSD possession	10.1 years	13.9 years
Attempted murder with harm	6.5	8.1
Rape	5.8	7.2
Armed robbery (gun)	4.7	5.9
Kidnapping	4.2	5.2
Theft of $80 million or more	4.2	5.2
Extortion	2.2	2.7
Burglary (carrying gun)	2.0	2.5
Taking a bribe	.5	1.0
Blackmail	.3	.8

Source: *United States Sentencing Guidelines Manual*; Drug Enforcement Administration.

A Psychedelic Quirk in the Law

Unlike other drugs such as heroin or cocaine, LSD isn't sold by weight due to its minuteness. Producers either sell the dose pure or put it on something like a piece of paper or sugar cube, which is where the quirk occurs because the Supreme Court decided Congress was allowed to sentence offenders by the weight of the drug including the package it is placed on. For instance, the sentence for 100 hits of LSD, worth about $100 is ten months, for pure LSD, five years if it's on paper, and sixteen years if it's on sugar cubes.

Source: Ibid.

Most Drug Traffickers Have It Easy

The average stay of 22 months for a drug trafficker is less than the average sentence for those convicted of aggravated assault or robbery.

Source: National Institute on Drug Abuse.

Sentencing of Drug Traffickers

Nationwide, state courts send 37 percent of drug traffickers to prison, 27 percent to local jails, and 35 percent to straight probation.

Source: National Judicial Reporting Program of the United States
Department of Justice.

Legally Drunk

A person who weighs 150 pounds and has had little or no food intake needs to consume about five ounces of 80-proof liquor in one hour to reach a blood-alcohol level of .10. Five ounces of alcohol is equivalent to four 12-ounce cans of beer or four 4-ounce glasses of wine.

Source: United States Department of Health and Human Services.

Serving Time for Tax Evasion

In 1992, 1,590 taxpayers received a prison sentence for criminal tax violations. Assuming that roughly 100 million taxpayers file tax returns, the odds of a taxpayer receiving a sentence are .0016 percent.

Source: National Taxpayers Union.

Complaints Against Lawyers

In 1988, about 93,000 complaints were filed against lawyers; about 40 percent of the clients complained about alcohol or drug dependencies.

Source: HALT, a Washington, D.C., legal reform group.

Expensive Law Enforcement

The United States spends some $50 billion a year (that's $240 per man, woman, and child) on all aspects of law enforcement. If the United States keeps throwing people in prison in the 1990s at the same rate as in the 1980s, some 250 new cells a day will be needed. That's at least $5 billion a year for construction costs alone.

Source: Norval Morris, a University of Chicago Law School Professor.

An Increase in Violent Crimes

The United States population has grown 41 percent since 1960, whereas violent crimes have increased 516 percent. Fewer than 35 Americans became the victims of violent criminals every hour in 1960. Currently, about 200 Americans are victimized every hour.

Source: FBI and United States census statistics.

Grand Larceny on a Grand Scale

President Ferdinand Marcos and his wife, Imelda, reportedly stole as much as $10 billion during their twenty-year rule of the Philippines. If these figures are true, it means $1,369,863 was taken out of the till every day for twenty years!

Source: Authors' calculations.

The United States Murder Capitals

The following table lists the highest rates of homicides per 100,000 people per year:

City	Rate
Washington, D.C.	70.4
Detroit	51.0
New Orleans	51.0
Dallas	37.2
Baltimore	34.8
Boston	31.8
Jacksonville	30.2
New York	29.4
Houston	29.0
Chicago	27.2

Figures for first six months of 1990 at an annual rate.
Source: New York City Police Department.

100 Billion Bail

The highest bail ever set was $100 billion on Jeffrey Marsh, Juan Mercado, Yolanda Kravitz, and Alvin Kravitz accused of armed robbery. The four defense attorneys at the Dade County

Courthouse, Miami, Florida, set the bail on October 16, 1989, with David L. Tobin as the presiding judge.

Source: *Guinness Book of Records*, New York: Bantam Books, 1992.

America's High Crime Rates

The following table shows the percentage of the population in different industrialized nations who said they were a victim of a crime in 1989.

Country	Percent Victimized
United States	28.8
Canada	28.1
Australia	27.8
Netherlands	26.8
Spain	24.6
Germany	21.9
France	19.4
United Kingdom	19.4
Belgium	17.7
Norway	16.5
Finland	15.9
Switzerland	15.6
Japan	9.3

Source: van Dijk, Jan J. M., et al., *Experiences of Crime Across the World*, 2nd ed., Deventer, The Netherlands: Kluwer, 1991, page 174.

Drunk Driving Deaths

The United States has by far the highest rate of drunk driving deaths per capita. This may be because we travel by car more than any other country, and we are fourth in alcohol consumption. The following table shows the number of deaths due to drunk driving, and the rate per 100,000 people, from 1983–1990:

Country	Number Killed	Number per 100,000
United States	22,083	8.8
Poland	1,614	4.4
West Germany	2,547	4.1
Denmark	191	3.7
Hungary	387	3.6
Austria	263	3.5
Switzerland	215	3.3
Finland	112	2.3
Yugoslavia	467	2.1
East Germany	309	1.9
Czechoslovakia	272	1.8
Netherlands	260	1.8
Sweden	95	1.1
Belgium	77	0.8
United Kingdom	379	0.7
Spain	174	0.5
Turkey	120	0.3

Source: Adrian, M., P. Jull, and R. Williams, *Statistics on Alcohol and Drug Abuse in Canada and Other Countries*, vol. 1; *Statistics on Alcohol Use*, vol. 2; *Statistics on Drug Use*, Toronto: Alcoholism and Drug Addiction Research Foundation, 1989, Table 1.29; United Nations; Mothers Against Drunk Driving (MADD).

Advertising Law

The following table shows which medium lawyers used to advertise in 1990, by percentage:

Medium	Percentage
Yellow Pages	90
Newspapers	20
Magazines or Journals	10
Radio	8
Direct Mail	7
Television	6

Source: Gellman, David, "Developing Your Firm's Advertising and Marketing Strategy," *Lawyers Alert,* May 14, 1990, page 19; Olson, Walter K., *The Litigation Explosion*, New York: Truman Talley, 1991, pages 16–24.

World's Largest Product-Liability Settlement

On September 1, 1994, U. S. District Judge Sam C. Pointer, Jr., in Birmingham, Alabama, gave final approval to a $4.2 billion settlement to women who suffered illnesses as a result of breast implants. Nearly all major suppliers, manufacturers, and distributors of breast implants are parties to the agreement. The leading corporate participants are Dow Corning Corp., a joint venture of Dow Chemical Co. and Corning Inc., Bristol-Myers Squibb Co., Baxter International Inc., Minnesota Mining & Manufacturing Co., and Union Carbide Corp. The settlement sets out differing levels of compensation payable over 30 years to women with various illnesses allegedly related to implants. An estimated 90, 000 women have registered to participate in the settlement.

Source: Burton, Thomas M., "Settlement Over Breast Implants Gets Final Approval From Judge," *Wall Street Journal,* Septmber 1, 1994, page B2.

The Worst and the Best States to Be Sued

Here is a list of the fifty states and the District of Columbia in descending order from most litigious to least litigious:

Rank	State
1	District of Columbia
2	Rhode Island
3	Massachusetts
4	New Mexico
5	Nevada
6	Delaware
7	Florida
8	New York
9	New Hampshire
10	Washington
11	New Jersey
12	Connecticut
13	California
14	Maryland
15	Illinois
16	Michigan
17	Pennsylvania
18	Texas
19	Louisiana
20	West Virginia

Rank	State
21	Maine
22	Georgia
23	Missouri
24	Hawaii
25	Vermont
26	Ohio
27	Alaska
28	Alabama
29	Kentucky
30	Arizona
31	Mississippi
32	Minnesota
33	Oklahoma
34	Virginia
35	North Carolina
36	Montana
37	Iowa
38	South Carolina
39	Wyoming
40	Wisconsin
41	Colorado
42	Tennessee
43	Oregon
44	Idaho
45	Nebraska
46	Arkansas
47	South Dakota
48	Kansas
49	North Dakota
50	Indiana
51	Utah

Source: Frum, David, and Frank Wolfe, "If You Gotta Get Sued, Get Sued in Utah," *Forbes*, January 17, 1994, pages 70–73.

$1 Million Awards

The following are the top ten states in which to sue for the highest award:

Rank	State	$1 Million Awards (1962–1989)
1	New York	707
2	California	540
3	Florida	504
4	Texas	320
5	Illinois	216
6	Michigan	202
7	Pennsylvania	177
8	Ohio	100
9	Missouri	96
10	New Jersey	86

Source: *The Lawyer's Almanac.*

Cutting Outside Legal Costs

In 1991, big companies cut their outside legal spending by 24 percent from 1990. Out of the Fortune 500 companies surveyed, median fees paid to outside vendors dropped from $7,432,000 in 1990 to $5,680,022 in 1991. Although some of the decrease is due to an increased spending on in-house lawyers, the survey found that companies still saved 15 percent on total legal costs.

Source: Price Waterhouse, survey of Fortune 500 companies.

Medical Malpractice Costs

The following three tables give the total number of medical malpractice verdicts and average verdicts for three classifications:

Classification Verdict	Year	Total Verdicts	Average
Doctors as Sole Defendant	1988	183	$730,575
	1989	216	$815,906
	1990	182	$1,105,257
Hospitals as Sole Defendant	1988	87	$1,497,037
	1989	77	$1,836,429
	1990	62	$1,761,838
Doctor and Hospital as Co-Defendants	1988	90	$1,483,060
	1989	130	$1,167,273
	1990	99	$2,975,945

Source: *The Lawyer's Almanac.*

Views on Separation of Church and State

The separation of church and state has been a huge controversy throughout the last decade. How do people really feel about it? The following questions were asked of 500 American adults from a telephone poll in 1991 by Yankelovich Clancy Shulman. (Sampling error is plus or minus 4.5 percent; "unsures" were omitted.)

The following table lists what percent of people surveyed thought that the following activities should be allowed on school grounds:

Activity	Yes Answers
Voluntary Bible classes	78%
Voluntary Christian fellowship groups	78
Prayers before athletic games	73
Church choir practice	56

The following table indicates the percent of people who favor and oppose the following activities.

Activity	Oppose	Favor
Allowing children to say prayers in public schools	18%	78%
Allowing children to spend a moment in silent meditation in public schools	9	89
Displaying symbols like a nativity scene or a menorah on government property	26	67
Removing references to God from all oaths of public office	74	20

When asked whether they would vote for a presidential candidate who did not believe in God, 63 percent of the people surveyed responded "no"; 29 percent responded "yes."

Famous Lawyers Who Never Went to Law School

1. Patrick Henry (1736–1799), member of the Continental Congress, governor of Virginia

2. John Jay (1745–1829), first chief justice of the Supreme Court

3. John Marshall (1755–1835), chief justice of the Supreme Court

4. William Wirt (1772–1834), attorney general

5. Roger B. Taney (1777–1864), secretary of the treasury, chief justice of the Supreme Court

6. Daniel Webster (1782–1852), secretary of state

7. Salmon P. Chase (1808–1873), senator, chief justice of the Supreme Court

8. Abraham Lincoln (1809–1865), president

9. Stephen Douglas (1813–1861), representative, senator from Illinois.

10. Robert Storey (b.1893), president of the American Bar Association (1952–1953)

11. J. Strom Thurmond (b. 1902), senator, governor of South Carolina

12. James O. Eastland (b. 1904), senator from Mississippi

Source: Wallace, Amy, Irving Wallace, and David Wallace, *The Book Of Lists #3*, New York: William Morrow & Company Inc., 1983.

Affirmative Action Legislation Not Needed

The following question was asked of 404 senior executives drawn from the *Business Week 1000* from June 10–14, 1991: "Do you feel that affirmative action laws on the hiring of women and minorities are needed, or do you think most companies such as yours would hire and train and give women and minorities the opportunity to get ahead without such laws?" Of the people surveyed, 31 percent thought affirmative action laws were needed; 65 percent thought businesses would do the job themselves; and 4 percent were unsure.

Juvenile Crime on the Rise

The number of arrests of juveniles in the United States has risen substantially since the early 1980s.

Type of Crime	1983	1992
Murder	1,175	2,680
Rape	3,914	4,882
Robbery	31,293	38,192
Assault	29,917	58,383
Burglary	138,591	111,385
Theft	320,614	362,066
Car Theft	31,857	70,201
Arson	5,626	7,094

Source: FBI uniform crime index.

New Laws—What's New?

Every year, Americans get 150,000 new laws from all levels of government—federal, state, and local—not to mention the 2 million new regulations every year.

Source: Asimov, Isaac, *Asimov's Book of Facts*, Mamaroneck, NY: Hasting House, 1992.

Law Enforcement Employees

There were an average of 2.8 law enforcement employees per 1,000 inhabitants for all cities nationwide in 1992.

Source: United States Department of Justice Statistics Bulletin, Uniform Crime Reports for the United States 1992.

Justice Spending

Federal, state, and local governments combined spent $299 per capita on criminal and civil justice in 1990. Across the nation, state and local governments spent $261 per capita on justice activities. This ranged from less than $100 per capita in West Virginia ($97) to more than $400 per capita in New York ($480) and Alaska ($608). Criminal justice spending includes funds spent on police protection, courts, prosecution and legal services, public defense, corrections, crime commissions, neighborhood crime councils, and state criminal justice crime councils.

Source: United States Department of Justice Statistics Bulletin, Justice Expenditure and Employment, 1990.

Sentencing Felons

In 1990, state courts sentenced 46 percent of convicted felons to state prison, 25 percent to local jail (usually for a year or less) and the remaining 29 percent to straight probation with no jail or prison time to serve. State courts sentenced to death only 2 percent of those convicted of murder.

Source: United States Department of Justice Statistics Bulletin, Felony Sentences in State Courts, 1990.

Guilty or Innocent

Of the total number of convicted felons in 1990, 91 percent pleaded guilty to their crime. The rest were found guilty at trial. The average time from arrest to sentencing in 1990 was about seven months.

Source: Ibid.

Race of Felons

Of the felons convicted nationally in 1990, 52 percent were Caucasian, 47 percent were African American, and 1 percent were of other races. Males consisted of 86 percent of the total. The average age of convicted felons was 29 years old.

Source: Ibid.

Time in Prison

In 1990, the average length of sentences to state prison was 6.25 years.

Source: Ibid.

Prison Sentencing

The amount of time felons actually serve in prison normally is only a fraction of their total sentence. There are two reasons why felons are in prison for a shorter time than their sentence. First, some states use indeterminate sentences, which allow judges to specify minimum and maximum sentence length. Judges depend on parole boards to determine when a prisoner will be released. Second, most states grant inmates an early release based on time credits for good behavior or special achievements. These reduced-time sentences allow correctional officials to manage the populations of the prisons. Felons receiving an early release usually serve the remaining portion of their sentences under supervision in the community.

Source: United States Department of Justice, Bureau of Statistics Bulletin, Felony Sentences in State Courts, 1990.

The Brady Bill

The "Brady Bill" contains a mandatory five-day waiting period for background checks on all handgun purchases. Named after James Brady, President Reagan's press secretary who was injured during John Hinkley's assassination attempt on Reagan, the Brady Bill went into effect on February 28, 1994. It will have little impact on states with stronger gun control laws.

Source: "ABC World News Tonight," February 28, 1994.

Crimes with Firearms

In 1991, firearms were involved in 64 percent of all murders, almost 40 percent of all robberies, and nearly 25 percent of all aggravated assaults known to police. As you can see from the table below, these figures represent sharp increases from 1986:

Crime	Number of Crimes in 1991	Number of Crimes Firearm Was Used	Percentage	Increase from 1986
Murder	25,000	16,000	64%	34%
Robbery	688,000	275,000	40%	49%
Aggravated Assault	1,093,000	262,000	24%	50%

Source: American Bar Association, The State of Criminal Justice (1993).

Arrests for Crimes

In 1991, there were nearly 15,000,000 estimated index offenses (index offenses consist of murder, forcible rape, robbery, aggravated assault, burglary, larceny-theft, and vehicle theft) and nearly 3,000,000 arrests for such offenses. Fewer than 20 percent of the offenders committing property crimes (consisting of burglary, larceny, and vehicle theft) were arrested; however, over 37 percent of offenders committing violent crimes (consisting of murder, forcible rape, robbery, and aggravated assault) were arrested.

Source: Ibid.

Adult Arrests

In 1991, there were nearly 12,000,000 adult arrests and over 750,000 state prisoners. Violent, serious property, and drug offenses accounted for over 25 percent of the arrests and over 90 percent of the prisoners.

Source: Ibid.

Correctional Supervision

In 1990, over 4.4 million individuals, or 2.3 percent of the United States adult population, were under some form of correctional supervision, including persons in jail or prison, on probation or on parole.

Source: Ibid.

Kennedy Assassination—Not a Federal Felony

When President John F. Kennedy was assassinated in 1963, it was not a federal felony to kill the president.

Source: Ibid.

The Cost of Crime in the United States

In 1991, the cost of crime in America was more than $19 billion.

Source: Bureau of Justice Statistics, National Crime Victimization Survey.

Teenage Victims of Violent Crime in the United States

In 1992, black teen-age males were victims of violent crimes at a rate of 113 per 1,000; the rate for white teen-age males was 90 per 1,000.

Source: Ibid.

Violent Crime Hits the Poor and African Americans the Hardest

In 1992, violent crime hit people with the lowest incomes hardest, with African Americans suffering the worst.

Income	Victims per 1,000 People
Less than $7,500	59
$7,500–9,999	42
$10,000–14,999	43
$15,000–24,999	31
$25,000–24,999	32
$30,000–49,999	25
$50,000 or more	20

Race	Victims per 1,000 People
White	30
Black	44
Other	28

Source: Justice Department.

Crime Victims During Two Last Decades

Between 1973 and 1992, 36.6 million Americans were victims of violent crime.

Source: Bureau of Justice Statistics, National Crime Victimization Survey.

Rise in Caseloads

Between 1984 and 1991, civil caseloads have risen 33 percent. Criminal caseloads have increased 24 percent, and juvenile caseloads 34 percent. Between 1985 and 1991, felony filings increased by 50 percent, and criminal appeals by 21 percent.

Source: *State Court Caseload Statistics*, Williamsburg, VA: National Center for State Courts.

New Cases Filed

More than 93 million new cases were filed in state courts, including the District of Columbia and Puerto Rico in 1991. This figure is actually down from a record high of 100.5 million in 1990. The decrease is mainly due to an 11 percent drop in the number of traffic cases as more courts route parking violations through an administrative process. Although a decline in traffic caseloads occurred, civil filings, including torts, contracts, domestic relations, real estate, and small claims, grew 3 percent to 18.9 million in 1991. Criminal filings in general jurisdiction courts (primarily felonies) grew 1 percent, but declined in limited jurisdiction courts, for a combined total of 12.4 million. In addition, 1.6 million new juvenile cases were filed and 60.1 million traffic or other ordinance violation cases.

Source: Ibid.

The Top Ten States for Civil Case Filings

In 1991, 18,971,437 civil cases were filed in state courts, including the District of Columbia and Puerto Rico. The following table lists the ten states with the most filings:

Rank	State	Number
1	California	1,906,188
2	New York	1,569,457
3	Virginia	1,427,105
4	Florida	924,067
5	Maryland	913,698
6	New Jersey	911,714
7	Texas	857,322
8	Ohio	853,533
9	Illinois	726,359
10	Michigan	725,517

Montana ranked last with 214,679 filings. When adjusted for population, Vermont's 6,747 civil filings per 100,000 residents was the median.

Source: Ibid.

Special Interests

The Association of Trial Lawyers of America, which consists of 60,000 members, spends more per member on political donations than any other major lobbying group, including the American Medical Association. The ATLA contributed $2.4 million to congressional candidates in the 1991–1992 campaign. In addition, thousands of its individual members contribute as well. The ATLA also hires expensive lobbyists and underwrites seemingly independent consumer organizations with parallel agendas.

Source: Schmitt, Richard B., "Trial Lawyers Glide Past Critics with Aid of Potent Trade Support," *The Wall Street Journal*, February 17, 1994, page 1.

Highest per Capita Rate of Incarceration

In 1990–1991, the United States ranked first in all industrialized nations for the highest per capita rate of incarceration per 100,000 population.

Rank	Nation	Rate
1	United States	455
2	South Africa	311
3	Venezuela	177
4	Hungary	117
5	Canada	111
5	China	111
7	Australia	79
8	Portugal	77
9	Czechoslovakia	72
10	Denmark	71
11	Albania	55
12	Netherlands	46
13	Republic of Ireland	44
13	Sweden	44
15	Japan	42
16	India	34

Source: Americans Behind Bars: One Year Later, The Sentencing Project, February 1992.

Trial by Jury

The "trial by jury of your peers" is predominantly an Anglo-American institution. About 120,000 jury trials are conducted each year in the United States—more than 90 percent of all jury trials in the world.

Source: Candisky, Catherine, and Randall Edwards, "Courting Jurors," *The Columbus Dispatch*, February 20, 1994, page 1A.

Population Boom

The number of adults in the criminal justice system more than doubled from 1980 to 1990, while the nation's total adult population rose 13 percent, and the number of adults arrested increased 34 percent.

Status	1980	1990	Percent Change
Jails	163,994	403,019	146
Parole	220,438	531,407	141
Probation	1,118,097	2,670,234	139
Prison	329,821	771,243	134
Total	1,832,350	4,375,903	139

Source: National Council on Crime and Delinquency, February 1993.

The High Cost of Crime

Crime costs America an estimated $425 billion a year. This figure comes from an analysis of all the direct and indirect costs of property and violent crimes. This cost includes everything from emergency room care for a mugging victim to the price of a new alarm system.

Source: "The Economics of Crime," *Business Week*, December 13, 1993.

Big Bills for Private Protection

An estimated $65 million a year is spent by businesses and consumers on private security, including alarms, guards, and locks.

Source: William Cunningham, president of Hallcrest Systems, Inc.

Violent Criminals at Large

In 1992, 1,932,000 violent crimes were reported to police. Of that only 742,000 people were arrested, and only 410,000 people were actually held for these violent crimes.

Source: Justice Department.

Drug Offenders Crowding Our Prisons

In 1993, about 60 percent of inmates in federal prisons and 20 percent of inmates in state prisons were there on drug charges.

Source: "The Economics of Crime," *Business Week*, December 13, 1993.

Where Orthopedic Surgeons Pay the Most and Least Malpractice Premiums

The annual premiums for malpractice insurance fluctuate considerably from state to state. The following table lists what premiums average on a state-by-state basis, with Michigan being the highest ($108,762 a year) and bordering Indiana ($4,350) being the lowest.

Rank	State	Average Malpractice Premium for Orthopedic Surgeon
1	Michigan	$108,762
2	Florida	73,788
3	New York	65,451
4	Rhode Island	46,045
5	Alaska	45,203
6	Massachusetts	36,190
7	California	35,218
8	New Mexico	30,770
9	Nevada	28,739
10	Washington, D.C.	25,023
11	Texas	24,868
12	Hawaii	24,500
13	Missouri	23,395
14	New Jersey	22,982
15	Arizona	22,307
16	Illinois	21,764
17	West Virginia	20,502
18	Maryland	19,287
19	Oklahoma	18,299
20	Washington	18,258
21	Ohio	17,366

Rank	State	Average Malpractice Premium for Orthopedic Surgeon
22	Connecticut	14,729
23	Delaware	14,079
24	Georgia	13,360
25	Mississippi	12,952
26	Alabama	12,860
27	North Dakota	12,032
28	Pennsylvania	11,904
29	Wyoming	11,549
30	New Hampshire	11,148
31	Colorado	10,943
32	Montana	10,889
33	Idaho	10,624
34	Oregon	10,415
35	Kentucky	10,383
36	Maine	10,050
37	Iowa	9,462
38	Vermont	8,564
39	Virginia	8,246
40	Wisconsin	8,111
41	Tennessee	8,057
42	Louisiana	7,937
43	Utah	7,597
44	Minnesota	7,537
45	North Carolina	7,320
46	South Carolina	6,497
47	Kansas	6,232
48	South Dakota	5,875
49	Arkansas	5,388
50	Nebraska	4,359
51	Indiana	4,350

Source: Frum, David, and Frank Wolfe, "If You Gotta Get Sued, Get Sued in Utah," *Forbes*, January 17, 1994, pages 72–73.

African Americans and Crime

Although African Americans make up only 12 percent of our nation's population, their share of crime arrests is much higher. Of all the arrests made in 1992, African Americans accounted for 55.1 percent of all murder and non-negligent manslaughter, 60.9 percent of all robbery, 38.8 percent of all aggravated assault, and 30.4 percent of all burglary arrests.

African Americans also make up 49 percent of the prison population; nearly one in four African Americans between the ages of 20 and 29 are in jail, on probation, or on parole.

Source: Federal Bureau of Investigation, The Sentencing Project.

More Firearms in Robberies

The number of firearms increased by 27 percent between the years from 1986 to 1991. During the same years, the use of firearms in robberies increased by 49 percent.

Source: "The Economics of Crime," *Business Week*, December 13, 1993.

Less Sympathetic Juries

According to a study of more than 90,000 cases, juries in 1992 sided with alleged personal-injury victims in about 52 percent of suits that went to trial. Five years previously, in 1987, juries sided with 61 percent. During the same five-year period, juries sided with plaintiffs in product liability suits 43 percent in 1992 as compared with 54 percent in 1987. In cases against consumer products manufacturers, consumers won only 39 percent of the cases in 1992 as compared with 55 percent in 1987.

Source: Jury Verdict Research, Horsham, Pennsylvania.

Malpractice Verdicts Down Against Doctors and Hospitals

In 1987, patients won 42 percent of the malpractice suits brought against doctors and 59 percent against hospitals versus 25 percent against doctors and 50 percent against hospitals in 1992.

Source: Ibid.

Public Believes Jury Awards Are too High

About 75 percent of jurors believe jury awards are too large, and an estimated 66 percent believe there are too many lawsuits.

Source: FTI Jury Analyst Group, Annapolis, Maryland; Felsenthal, Edward, "Jury Displays Less Sympathy in Injury Claims," *Wall Street Journal*, March 21, 1994, page B1.

Yale Law School—A Long Shot to Get In

Yale Law School, ranked number one according to a *U.S. News & World Report* survey, received 4,949 applications and admitted 286 new students, or 6 percent. (Of those that applied, the odds were 16.6 to 1 of getting in—and only top students need bother to submit an application.) The typical successful candidate has a GPA of 3.8 and a score of 171 on the Law School Admission Test.

Source: "A Long Shot at Best," *U.S. News & World Report*, March 21, 1994, page 72.

Biggest Law Firm Bankruptcy

In 1988, Finley, Kumble, Wagner, Heine, Underberg, Manley, Myerson & Casey, once America's fourth largest law firm with 700 attorneys, filed bankruptcy. The New York law firm had $105 million of debt, excluding malpractice claims. It was the biggest law firm bankruptcy ever.

Meanwhile, the bankruptcy has enriched the professionals picking at the firm's carcass, including lawyers, trustees, and accountants, who have received fees in excess of $37 million. Anyone who lent the firm a significant sum of money, including ending banks, hasn't received a dime, however. It is estimated that bank creditors lent Finley Kumble a total of $85 million. To date, Milbank, Tweed, Hadley & McCloy, a New York law firm, has received $23 million in fees.

The Federal Deposit Insurance Corporation, the successor to one of Finley Kumble's lenders, has a $10.4 million claim of which it anticipates receiving about 20 cents on the dollar. The bankruptcy is expected to be completely wrapped up around the year 2000.

Source: Stevens, Amy, "Finley Kumble's Creditors Left Wanting but Bankruptcy Pros Collect Their Fees," *Wall Street Journal*, April 8, 1994, page B1.

Long Hours

Thirteen percent of lawyers in private practice claim to have worked more than 240 hours a month in 1990, compared with 4 percent in 1984.

Source: American Bar Association.

Billable Hours

It was recently reported that a top partner in a respected Chicago law firm charged clients for 6,022 hours of work in 1993. These "billable hours" amount to a work day of 16.5 hours a day, seven days a week, every week of the year. Such an output is virtually impossible. Although most big firms typically expect lawyers to bill 1,700 to 2,200 hours a year, annual billings of even 3,000 hours a year are very rare.

Records of this partner's personal billings to clients raise questions about prior year billings as well. In the three previous years, he billed an average of $1.7 million, which included 5,000 billable hours each year at a billable rate of approximately $350 an hour.

A lawyer's billable time should consist only of time spent on a client's behalf. Billable time does not include vacations, sleeping, trips to and from the office, or bathroom breaks. An internal memorandum from this partner's firm specifies that "firm management, departmental, client relations/business development, general office" matters are not billable.

Although lawyers familiar with the accused partner describe him as a tenacious litigator who regularly puts in long days and weekends at the office embroiled in complex business disputes, no person could possibly explain how he spent all of his time while he was awake on billable matters!

Source: *Wall Street Journal*, May 27, 1994, page B1.

Busy Associate Lawyers Equal More Bucks for Law Partners

In a 1990 study, a partner at a law firm where associates bill 2,100 hours a year will earn $84,000 more than a partner at a firm where associates bill 1,500 hours a year.

Source: Study by Dr. Susan Samuelson, Boston University School of Management.

Profitable Law Firms

The top 15 law firms in *The American Lawyer* magazine's "Top 100," ranked by profits per partner in 1993, were:

Firm	Profits for Partner	Size Lawyers	Partners
Cravath, Swaine & Moore	$1,410,000	280	73
Wachtell, Lipton, Rosen & Katz	1,350,000	103	54
Sullivan & Cromwell	1,275,000	374	101
Cahill Gordon & Reindel	1,210,000	201	54
Davis Polk & Wardwell	1,020,000	404	97
Simpson Thacher & Bartlett	925,000	377	98
Cleary, Gottlieb, Steen & Hamilton	890,000	464	119
Weil, Gotshal & Manges	745,000	635	150
Wilkie Farr & Gallagher	720,000	326	106
Kirkland & Ellis	700,000	390	95
Skadden, Arps, Slate, Meagher & Flom	690,000	948	222
Debevoise & Plimpton	685,000	325	81
Williams & Connolly	635,000	141	59
Paul, Weiss, Rifkind, Wharton & Garrison	610,000	333	89
Shearman & Sterling	590,000	512	132

Source: *Wall Street Journal*, June 30, 1994, page B-5.

Doctors Outwork Lawyers

Fifty-three percent of America's full-time lawyers put in more than 50 hours a week in 1992, compared with 72 percent of physicians.

Source: Bureau of Labor Statistics.

High Cost of Crime-Related Injuries

A single crime-related injury costs an average of $41,000 for medical and psychological problems. It is estimated that the injury-causing crimes that occur in a single year in the United States and the bill to society—in medical, psychological, and productivity losses—ultimately is $202 billion over the victims' lifetimes.

Source: *Health Affairs*, 1994.

Millions of Americans Hurt by Crime

Nearly 37 million people have been injured by criminals in the United States during the past 20 years. And, although over-all crime is down 6 percent over the past 20 years, violence is up 24 percent partly because of attacks on African Americans.

Source: Justice Department, 1993.

Gun Laws Vary According to State

Only 26 states and the District of Columbia have restrictions on the purchase of weapons. These restrictions could involve a wait before purchase, a wait before a background check, and in some cases, a cooling off period after a background check.

State	Wait	Weapon	Background Check	Cooling Off Period
Alabama	48 hours	Handguns	No	No
California	15 days	All firearms	No	No
Connecticut	14 days	All firearms	No	No
Delaware	3 days	Handguns and rifles	Yes	No
Washington, D.C.	None	Shotguns and rifles (no handgun sales permitted)	Yes	No
Florida	3 business days	All firearms	Yes	No
Hawaii	15 days*	All firearms	Yes	No
Illinois	30 days*	All firearms	Yes	1–3 days
Iowa	3 days*	Handguns	Yes	3 days
Maryland	7 days	Handguns and assault weapons	No	No
Massachusetts	40 days*	All firearms	Yes	No
Michigan	None	Handguns	Yes	No
Minnesota	7 days	Handguns	No	No
Missouri	7 business days	Handguns	Yes	No
Nebraska	2 business days*	Handguns	Yes	No
New Jersey	30 days*	All firearms	Yes	No
New York	6 months*	Handguns	Yes	No
North Carolina	30 days*	Handguns	Yes	No
Oregon	15 days	Handguns	No	No
Pennsylvania	48 hours	Handguns	No	No

State	Wait	Weapon	Background Check	Cooling Off Period
Rhode Island	7 days	All firearms	No	No
South Dakota	48 hours	Handguns	No	No
Tennessee	15 days	Handguns	No	No
Virginia	48 hours**	All firearms	Yes	No
Washington	5 days	Handguns	No	No
Wisconsin	5 days*	Handguns	Yes	No

*maximum
**estimated

Source: *USA Today*, December 29, 1993.

Guns by the Numbers in the United States

- In the United States, 211 million firearms exist—enough to arm every adult and more than half the children.

- 12,489 people were slain with handguns in 1992, nearly twice the number of fatal shootings in 1966.

- 15,377 people lost their lives in all firearm homicides, including rifles and shotguns, in 1992.

- 1,004 people were shot to death at work in 1992—17 percent of the total workplace deaths of 6,083.

- Sixteen mass killings with firearms in 1992 left 62 people dead—including nine attackers—and 51 wounded.

- 780 more people died in gun suicides (18,526) in 1991 than gun homicides.

- Seven out of ten homicides in the United States in 1992 were a result of firearms.

- 269,000 businesses—from retail stores to pawn brokers—are licensed to sell firearms.

- 1,791 federally licensed gun dealers operated in Houston in 1991, the most in the United States.

- 4,505 handguns, on average, were sold in California in the days after the acquittal of four Los Angeles police officers in the Rodney King beating.

- 240 Federal Bureau of Alcohol, Tobacco and Firearms agents are responsible for inspecting the nation's gun shops—an average of 1,100 shops per agent.

- One in ten Americans now lives in community "crime watch" neighborhoods.

- Americans are fifteen times more likely to be killed by gunfire than Europeans.

- Twenty years, three months is the average sentence handed out for murder.

- Eight years, eight months is the average time served for murder.

- 28 percent of state inmates say they got guns "on the street."

- Every 52 hours a police officer is killed.

- 925,247 people are in federal and state prisons.

- $22,400 is the average cost of keeping a federal prisoner for one year.

- 52 percent of the inmates convicted of a violent crime say they used a gun merely to scare their victims.

- 83 percent of male inmates under 18 say they had a gun at home.

- $65 billion is being spent by United States businesses for security, up 25 percent since 1990.

Source: *USA Today* research; Bureau of Alcohol, Tobacco, and Firearms; Justice Department's Bureau of Justice Statistics; Time Mirror Center for The People and The Press.

Trademark Names That Have Become Generic

Trademark laws insist that if you have a trademark, you must protect it and stop others from using it. Consequently, if somebody else uses your trademark and you don't notify the other party that he or she has infringed on your trademark, it becomes public domain. This means that anyone can then use it. Many trademarked products have become generic in this way.

Sometimes companies do their job of creating a public awareness of their trademark so well that everybody uses it as a common word to identify the product. After a trademarked product becomes a generic word, the trademark is no longer valid. For example, when you have a headache, you simply ask for an aspirin; but at one time it was a trademarked brand name of Bayer. Now that the word has become generic, Bayer does not have an exclusive right to use the word *aspirin* for its product.

The following products were at one time registered with the U.S. Patent and Trademark Office, but are now referred to in everyday speech to describe an entire category of merchandise rather than a specific product of a manufacturer.

•**Aspirin.** Astonishingly enough, the name of the pain reliever was once a trademark of Bayer. Originally, Bayer manufactured a product called acetylsalicylic acid, but that name was too difficult for people to pronounce and remember. So in 1899, Bayer changed the name to Aspirin. The name caught on very well—so well that it became generic through everyday use.

•**Cellophane.** Cellophane was once a trademark of Du Pont de Nemours and Company, who began to use the coined name in describing wrapping paper, sometimes making reference to a class of cellulose products, not as a unique brand name that it exclusively produced. When a competitor used the word *cellophane* to describe its product, Du Pont objected and took the company to court. Du Pont lost the case and thereby freed the word to enter the public domain.

•**Corn flakes and other breakfast cereal.** Corn flakes, raisin bran, and shredded wheat were brand names of Kellogg's, Post, and Nabisco respectively. Now any cereal company can use these terms.

•**Dry Ice.** Dry ice, a refrigerant, was once a registered trademark of the Dry Ice Corporation, but is now a generic term. Its scientific name is solidified carbon dioxide.

•**Escalator.** The moving stairway known as an escalator was once used exclusively by the Otis Elevator Company, but is no longer a trade name.

•**Linoleum.** Linoleum was a trademark name of Armstrong Cork Company that has become a generic word for this type of floor covering.

•**Murphy Bed.** The Murphy Door Bed Company, the original maker of Murphy beds, saw its product become a common term because it did not protect the name as a trademark. Now, a bed that folds up into the closet is a Murphy bed regardless of who manufactures it.

•**Nylon.** Nylon was once a registered trademark of Du Pont, but has since become a generic word for this synthetic fiber.

•**Thermos.** Thermos was once a trademark of the King-Seeley Thermos Company, but is now used to describe any type of vacuum flask that keeps food or liquid warm or cold.

•**Trampoline.** Although trampoline was once a brand name, it is now used generically by all manufacturers to describe the tautly stretched, springy mount used for aerial aerobatics.

•**Yo-yo.** Believe it or not, yo-yos were once a trademark of the Louis Marx Company when they were first on the market.

•**Zipper.** This word was once a registered trademark of B. F. Goodrich, but has since become a generic term for any of the interlocked fasteners.

Source: Shook, Michael D., *By Any Other Name*, New York: Macmillan, 1994, page 240.

Trademark Names

The following trademarked names are commonly thought to be generic, but are not:

•**Band-Aid.** This product was introduced in 1921 by Johnson & Johnson. Although we tend to refer to all adhesive bandages by this name, Band-Aid is a trademark name.

•**Jeep.** Although many off-road and utility vehicles are called Jeeps, a Jeep is a registered trademark of the Chrysler Corporation.

•**Kleenex.** Kleenex is a trademark registered with Kimberly-Clark, not just any tissue handkerchief.

•**Scotch Tape.** Although many people ask for Scotch Tape when they want clear adhesive tape, Scotch Transparent Tape is manufactured only by the Minnesota Mining and Manufacturing Company.

•**Vaseline.** This petroleum jelly product is a registered trademark of Cheseborough-Pond's.

•**Xerox.** Although used commonly as both a noun and a verb to denote a photocopy or making a photocopy, Xerox is a registered trademark of the Xerox Corporation.

Source: Ibid.

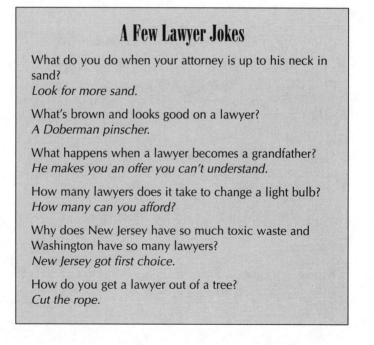

A Few Lawyer Jokes

What do you do when your attorney is up to his neck in sand?
Look for more sand.

What's brown and looks good on a lawyer?
A Doberman pinscher.

What happens when a lawyer becomes a grandfather?
He makes you an offer you can't understand.

How many lawyers does it take to change a light bulb?
How many can you afford?

Why does New Jersey have so much toxic waste and Washington have so many lawyers?
New Jersey got first choice.

How do you get a lawyer out of a tree?
Cut the rope.

What's the difference between a lawyer and an onion?
When you cut the onion, you cry.

What do you call an empty seat on a bus full of lawyers that goes off a cliff?
A wasted opportunity.

What's the difference between a pothole and a lawyer?
You swerve to avoid a pothole.

What's the difference between a lawyer and a sperm?
At 1,000,000 to 1 odds, a sperm has a better chance to be a human being.

What do you call 1,000 lawyers in cement blocks at the bottom of the sea?
A good start.

Why do they bury lawyers in 12-foot graves?
Because deep down, lawyers are good.

What does a lawyer use as a contraceptive?
His personality.

What is the difference between a lawyer and a vampire bat?
One is a blood sucking parasite, and the other is a mouselike creature with wings.

What is the difference between a hooker and a lawyer?
There are some things a hooker won't do for money.

What is a lawyer?
Someone who makes sure he gets what's coming to you.

Traffic Court

More than half the time in United States courts is spent on cases involving automobiles.

Source: Asimov, Isaac, *Asimov's Book of Facts*, Mamaroneck, NY: Hasting House, 1992, page 199.

America: A Land of Laws and Regulations

An estimated 150,000 new laws and two million law regulations are passed from all levels of government—federal, state, and local—in the United States.

Source: Ibid., page 197.

What a Difference a Comma Makes

In 1850, the state of Michigan wrote a law into its constitution reading: "Neither slavery nor involuntary servitude, unless for the punishment of crime, shall ever be tolerated in this state." To be grammatically correct, a comma should have followed the word *slavery* in the sentence. Without the comma, slavery was legal as an appropriate punishment for crime. In 1963, 113 years later, a comma was added, and only then was slavery (grammatically) outlawed in Michigan!

Source: Ibid., page 198.

Why Are They Called "Blue Laws"?

Back in 1665, Theophilus Eaton, the governor of the New Haven Colony, and John Davenport, a clergyman, drew up a strict legal code regulating personal conduct, later known as "Blue Laws." The name was given because the laws were printed on blue paper.

Source: Ibid., page 199.

Why Do We Say "Red Tape"?

The term "red tape" refers to official inaction or delay caused by bureaucratic shuffle (most notably by government institutions and big business). It originated in England in the nineteenth century when it was customary to tie official and legal documents with a tape of a pinkish red color. Harassed by officials who delayed government decisions by giving them undue attention to routine and hiding behind excuses for their rules and regulations, the common man ridiculed the process of tying and untying the red tape that bound the dispatch and document cases in public offices.

Source: Shook, Michael D., *The Book of Why*, Maplewood, NJ: Hammond Incorporated, 1983, page 63.

Blue Sky Laws

The Kansas legislature passed the first blue sky law in 1911. During this period of speculation, the Kansas secretary of state required investment companies to file a full description of their business activities, and until authorized by the state bank commissioner, their securities could not be sold. One member of the legislature declared that if given the opportunity, the wildcat promoters would capitalize the blue skies. Another legislator then argued that the restrictions on investment firms should be "as far-reaching as the blue sky." Hence, the saying "blue sky laws."

Source: Ibid., page 68.

Hello Officer

State police are no "dummies" when it comes to being creative in catching speeding motorists. But that trooper along Interstate 95 is a "dummy." Due to an inadequate number of police officers in Cecil County, Maryland, the police department enlisted the help of two female mannequins donated by a clothing store. The mannequins are dressed in trooper uniforms and are propped up in the driver's seat of old patrol cars. The dummy cars have been stationed for intervals at various spots along the 53-mile stretch of Interstate 95 between the Baltimore Beltway and the Delaware State border. The dummy cars have caused speeding drivers to slow down. Once speeding drivers caught onto these cars, police continued their creative touch. The police force has been periodically tossing the mannequin in the back seat and putting a real trooper in its place, or setting a speed trap a little farther down the road.

Source: *The Washington Times*, August 30, 1993, page B2.

Dishonest References

Only 55 percent of former employers are totally honest when they give references on ex-employees. Their lies are blamed on fear of lawsuits.

Source: Robert Half International, 1994.

Chapter 3

THE LAWS OF THE LAND IN OTHER LANDS

The United States is by no means the only nation with farcical legislation on the books—it's a worldwide phenomenon. This chapter is full of loony laws from around the world.

Only seeing-eye dogs are allowed in Reykjavik, Iceland.

It is against the law in Quebec to deliver milk before 7 A.M.

Wearing white shoes is against the law in Tibet.

It is against the law in Para, Brazil, to sing in the streets.

In Toronto, Canada, it is against the law to run for a streetcar.

Marriage to a goat is legal for women in India.

An old British law permits a man to beat his wife as long as the weapon is not larger than his little finger.

Nude sunbathing, even in one's backyard, is against the law in Canada.

In Britain, it is against the law for one member of parliament to insult another.

You must be literate in order to get married in Finland.

In Italy, it is against the law for a wife to rest her head on her husband's shoulder while he is driving.

In London, you are allowed to be nude in a theater as long as you don't move a muscle.

Donald Duck comic books were banned in Finland because authorities thought it wasn't good to show children a hero who ran around without pants on.

It is illegal to sell antifreeze to Indians in Quebec, Canada.

In Sweden, it is unlawful for parents to insult or shame their children.

Some South Sea island chiefs reserve certain words in their language for themselves, and nobody else is permitted to use them.

It is against the law to name your child Monica in Equatorial Guinea.

In Charlottetown, England, liquor can only be bought with a prescription from your family doctor saying it is for medical uses only.

A man is breaking the law in Argentina if he kisses his wife in public.

The Laws of Singapore

Ever since the caning of Michael Fay, the world has focused on Singapore's system of suppressing dissent. Fay, an 18-year-old at the time, pleaded guilty to spray-painting cars. He claimed to confessing during interrogation because the police bullied him, threatened beatings, and deprived him of sleep. Fay was sentenced to four months in jail, a $2,200 fine, and caning by six lashes (which was later reduced to four). Caning entails a martial arts professional wielding a long rattan cane, which has been soaked in water, on the buttocks of a criminal. Skin and blood fly on the first stroke, and prisoners sometimes go into shock. Those who pass out are revived before the slashing is resumed.

There are many punishing laws in Singapore. Gum is forbidden because it taints the dirt-free environment. *Cosmopolitan* magazine is banned because its message corrupts women. Those failing to flush a public toilet after using it can be fined $90. Urine sensors in elevators detect those who cannot control their bladders and automatically lock the doors to seal in the perpetrator until police arrive. Homosexuality is also illegal. People convicted of possession of two kilograms or more of marijuana are electrocuted.

As a result of these laws, Singapore has little crime and is clean and orderly with a high standard of living. But many personal freedoms are sacrificed.

Sources: *St. Petersburg Times*, May 1, 1994, page 2; *Star Tribune*, May 3, 1994, page 13A.

It is against the law in China to use the color purple except for mourning.

In the Province of Crodosa, Argentina, it is illegal for a store owner to have show windows that "exhibit underwear in a provoking or shocking form."

In Grande Prairie, Alberta, all cats must wear a bell.

The governor is the only person on Barbados who is allowed to have a house with more than 100 windows.

Boxing is considered a brutal sport and is outlawed in the People's Republic of China.

Female sports players are required by law to wear cotton stockings in Australia.

In New Zealand, all dog owners are required by law to walk their dogs at least once every twenty-four hours.

Wardens in Sydney, Australia, must make their nightly rounds in bedroom slippers.

According to a seventeenth-century English law, bachelors and widowers over the age of twenty-five were taxed one shilling each year while they remained unmarried.

Norway has a law that prohibits cutting down a tree unless three saplings are planted in its place.

Pedestrians are required by law to walk on the right side of the walk and give hand signals before turning in Toronto, Canada.

Using headlights when driving a car at night is against the law in Beijing, China. It is feared that the lights may blind bicycle riders.

In Vienna, Austria, the law prohibits posters that show a woman's legs in any area where minors under the age of sixteen can see them.

It is illegal to wear short pants in the African nation of Malawi.

In London, England, it is against the law to drive a car without sitting in the front seat.

It is also illegal in London to kiss a girl on Sunday.

In Denmark, a twelve-year-old child has the right to consent to his or her adoption.

A person must have a license to sell garter snakes or elks' teeth in Manitoba, Canada.

In Australia, it is against the law to employ a woman under the age of forty-five as a chorus girl.

It is illegal to shake dust out of windows in Outremont, Quebec.

The use of handcuffs is prohibited in Brazil.

In Caracas, Venezuela, cars must honk their horns at every intersection.

It is illegal to double park a horse in Canmore, Alberta.

Carrying a white rooster while passing through the town of Kiluken, Liberia, is unlawful.

In Japan, nobody but the imperial family is permitted to drive a maroon car.

In Halifax, England, it is against the law to walk on a tightrope over the main streets of the city.

Catching a fish with an unbaited hook is illegal in the Yukon.

A Bulgaria law requires a man to have one rooster for every twelve hens in his flock and one gander for every three geese.

It is illegal for a child over the age of six to appear in public without wearing a shirt on the South Pacific island of Tonga.

In Montreal, Canada, it is against the law to water a garden when it is raining.

Making love in railway trains, buses, parked motorcars, churchyards, chapels, or parks is against the law in London, England.

Under Turkish law, it is policy to drop off a drunk driver in the countryside a distance of twenty miles, and he must walk back while under the watchful eye of a police escort.

In Quebec, you must be at least sixteen years old to go to a theater.

The laws against adultery among some Bantu tribes are so harsh that a man can be put to death for merely brushing against another man's wife as they walk by each other.

In Australia, a drunk driver's name is sent to the local newspapers with a public announcement under this headline: "He's drunk and in jail."

In Ecuador, a woman in childbirth is removed from the house while the father-to-be is treated with food, honored, and pampered until he recovers from the shock of becoming a father.

Before entering office in High Wycombe, England, it is the law for the new mayor to be weighed.

In Italy, kissing in public is only legal at railroad stations.

After fathering three children in Uttar Pradesh, India, the law requires a man to be sterilized. If the man does not voluntarily comply, he is imprisoned for two years during which time he will be sterilized. If he objects to this procedure, he is immediately castrated.

In Edmonton, Alberta, it is illegal to grow moss on rooftops.

In China, all relatives of a criminal may be beheaded.

In modern-day Egypt, a belly dancer who performs in public places must have her navel covered with gauze.

In ancient Egypt, courts of law met in the dark so that the judge could remain impartial by not seeing the defendant, accuser, or the witnesses.

It is against the law to rescue a drowning person in China because it is believed that it would interfere with his or her fate.

It is against the law for a woman to massage a male customer at a massage parlor in Edmonton, Alberta.

Flying kites is against the law in China.

Selling cigarette lighters is illegal in Nicaragua.

In Greece, a man cannot falsely promise to marry a girl in order to seduce her. If he does and she has intercourse with him, he must compensate her financially for the premarital loss of her virginity.

A law prohibits wearing sport shirts with zipper fronts in Havana, Cuba.

In Venezuela, love letters can be sent at half the rate if they are mailed in bright red envelopes.

It is illegal to kiss a person who is not a relative in Egypt.

In Montreal, Quebec, it is against the law to take up more than one space on a park bench.

In France, a man who is sentenced to be hanged can be reclaimed by a virtuous maiden who will marry him.

Wrestling with an untrained bull in public is illegal in England.

It is illegal to sing in a bar in Alberta, Canada.

Carrying a wheelbarrow along a sidewalk in Newfoundland is illegal.

In Campbell River, British Columbia, it is illegal to feed any pigeons you don't own.

In India, no woman can give evidence in Hindu courts of justice.

Jailers must bring imprisoned debtors a beer on demand in British Columbia.

Garbage cans must not be filled higher than three inches below the rim in Fredericton, New Brunswick.

It is against the law in England to share a taxi.

Sunday newspapers are not permitted in Ireland.

When a dog barks at night in Japan, his owner is sentenced to work for whomever it disturbed.

In Saskatchewan, it is unlawful to sell milk fresh from the cow.

In Chester, England, it is unlawful for a man not to raise his hat when a funeral passes.

The criminal code of Japan outlaws all public demonstrations of affection. Kissing a girl in public can result in a jail sentence.

In the Northwest Territories of Canada, it is illegal to keep chickens in the same shed as a milk cow.

The Kaffir tribe in South Africa prohibits a man from looking at his mother-in-law; likewise, a mother-in-law is violating the law if she goes where he might see her.

It is against the law for married couples to have more than one child in China.

In Shanghai, it is illegal to own a red car. By law your car must be painted the color assigned to your profession.

It is unlawful to put your feet on the seat next to yours while traveling on a train in Italy.

While a woman is giving birth to a child in Japan, the father must get in bed and simulate labor.

In Madrid, Spain, newspapers are not permitted to publish pictures of girls in bathing suits.

False teeth are outlawed in Switzerland.

In Baluchistan, a province of Pakistan, a man can legally acquire a wife by exchanging his sister for the woman he wants.

It is illegal for an Egyptian girl to marry a foreigner if there is more than twenty-five years' difference in their ages.

It is against the law for a man to knit during the fishing seasons on the island of Jersey.

In the tiny Himalayan state, Swat, a person found guilty of jaywalking is forced to run along the road until he falls over from total exhaustion.

Swedish law forbids teenage girls from taking full-length photographs of themselves in coin-operated photomats found in bus, subway, and train stations. Nude photographs from either the waist up or the waist down, however, are legal.

In the Cautin province of Chile, it is against the law to display pinups in the house. The military governor decried: "It is more worthwhile to admire a good landscape than a photograph of a nude woman."

It is illegal for an operator of a motor vehicle to drive with his or her arm resting on the window of the opening door in Durban, South Africa.

In Athens, Greece, a driver can lose his or her license if caught operating a motor vehicle on the public roads while "poorly dressed" or "unbathed."

It is illegal to mention Vitamin E on food labels in Canada.

You can be fined for telling a fairy story over the phone in England.

In Vancouver, British Columbia, riding a tricycle faster than ten miles per hour is prohibited by law.

The ability to read and write is mandatory by law in order to attend a dance or party in Navalocan, Spain.

In the former Soviet Union, fishing without a license was punishable by death.

Using music to advertise a business is illegal in Montreal, Quebec.

If a husband fails to keep his wife supplied with coffee in Saudi Arabia, she has the legal grounds for a divorce.

In Teruel, Spain, hitting a man with an egg, bottle, or cucumber is against the law.

You cannot lawfully use pennies to pay any debt over 25 cents in Canada.

It is against the law in Japan for children to throw away broken dolls.

In Tabasco, Mexico, jazz music is barred by law.

Staring at the mayor is illegal in Paris, France.

If the driver of a car gets into an accident in Rio de Janeiro and can dodge the police for twenty-four hours, he or she cannot be jailed pending trial.

It is against the law to eavesdrop in restaurants or on buses in England.

In Montreal, Quebec, it is against the law to sell crooked wood.

It is illegal to make the chief of police pay to play billiards in New Brunswick.

Dogs can legally run at large in the winter, but not in the summer in Bridgewater, Nova Scotia.

Brides who keep the clergy waiting to perform the ceremony in Bilston, England are fined.

Chapter 4

STRANGE AND UNUSUAL CASES

Has a court's decision ever shocked you? Out of the thousands of lawsuits filed each year, many verdicts handed down by our judicial system stagger the imagination. Of course, this is why courts exist in the first place. If all the decisions were obvious, we would not need judges and courts. Just the same, some rulings surprise even the most jaded jurists.

The following verdicts are such head-shakers. The names and places have been changed to protect the innocent (or guilty) parties: Nonetheless, they are based on actual decisions of United States courts. Also included are some verbatim excerpts proving that defendants can sometimes surpass the courts in unintended humor.

The Suicidal House Guest

While Barry and Pam Simpson were on vacation, they let John Wilson spend the night at their house. Upon their return, the Simpsons found John lying dead in the kitchen. John had slit his throat. The Simpsons were so violently sickened and upset that they sued John's estate for damages for shock and nervousness. The court ruled in their favor because John should have anticipated the effect his suicide would have on his hosts.

Source: LaVallient and Theroux, *What's the Verdict?* New York: Sterling Publishing Company, 1991.

The Late Pizza Delivery

Domino's Pizza, Inc. dropped its 30-minute delivery guarantee after being ordered to pay a $79 million judgment in a personal injury lawsuit involving one of its drivers. After a two-week trial, a St. Louis jury awarded $750,000 in actual damages and $78 million in punitive damages to a woman who suffered head and spinal cord injuries when a Domino's delivery van ran a red light and hit her car. It was speculated that the punitive damages were imposed to prevent negligent driving to meet the 30-minute deadline and to send a message to Domino's to discontinue this policy. A $79 million penalty is a strong message!

Sources: *Newsday*, January 2, 1994, page 29; *New York Law Journal*, February 25, 1994, page 3.

The Forged Warrant

Police obtained a search warrant to search Scott's house, believing that he had heroin in his possession. Scott's door had an outer iron gate that could be locked until he decided whether to allow a visitor to enter his home. The police conjectured that if they told Scott about the warrant, he might leave the gate locked and destroy the evidence. So they forged an arrest warrant on fictitious traffic offenses and showed it to Scott. Scott let the police in to clear up the "mistake." After they entered the house, the police showed Scott the true search warrant and found heroin.

In court, Scott's defense was that the search was illegal. However, Scott was found guilty because the police didn't rely on the fake warrant to make the arrest. The deception at the house did not violate Scott's constitutional rights.

Source: La Vallient and Theroux, *What's the Verdict?* New York: Sterling Publishing Company, 1991.

The Missing Security Guard

Alice went shopping at a convenience store operated by ABC Corporation and parked in its well-lighted parking lot. Upon returning to her car, Alice was mugged and sustained multiple injuries. The preceding year seven other muggings had occurred in the store's parking lot, so ABC Corporation had hired a security guard. During Alice's assault, however, he was inside the store. Alice sued ABC Corporation for failure to warn and for failure to provide adequate security. The court ruled in Alice's favor because it is a store owner's duty to provide a reasonably safe place for customers to shop.

Source: Ibid.

The Unfit Policeman

Clint, a police officer, was required by the police department to carry his gun at all times within city limits. One day when he came home after work, he shot his wife and committed suicide. His wife suffered brain damage and sued the police department for negligence. She argued that the police department failed to adopt an effective program of psychological screening of police officers. The department had tried several psychological tests in an effort to screen out emotionally unstable officers, but these had proven ineffective and had been abandoned. With no screening, it follows that any disturbed officer would be required to carry a gun at all times. The court found the police department guilty of negligence because it is reasonably foreseeable that such an officer might injure members of his family.

Source: Ibid.

The Innocent Observer

Kent never paid his traffic tickets, and several warrants for his arrest were issued. One day when his car was parked in front of Anna's house, the police knocked at Anna's door and asked for Kent. Anna said that she had never heard of him. Undeterred, the police looked through a window and noticed Kent hiding in the basement. They arrested him. Anna was charged with hampering or impeding a public official in the performance of his lawful duties. Anna, however, was found not guilty because her answer did not interrupt the progress of the police toward their objective.

Source: Ibid.

Shoe Fetish

A man who had a "love affair" with certain personal items of Marla Trump, wife of Donald Trump, was sentenced to up to four and one-half years in jail for stealing her shoes and lingerie. The man admitted to having a "sexual relationship" with Mrs. Trump's shoes. He was convicted of stealing her shoes, underwear, and other personal items to appease a clothing and shoe fetish.

Sources: _The Orlando Sentinel_, February 17, 1994, page A2; _The Orlando Sentinel_, April 8, 1994, page A2.

Car Trouble

Excuses, excuses. It seems when people get into traffic accidents, they can come up with some doozies. Here's what some actual defendants stated in courts.

The guy was all over the road. I had to swerve a number of times before I hit him.

The pedestrian had no idea which direction to go, so I ran over him.

The other car collided with mine without giving warning of its intentions.

In my attempt to kill a fly, I drove into a telephone pole.

A truck backed through my windshield into my wife's face.

I told the police that I was not injured, but on removing my hat, I found that I had a skull fracture.

I pulled away from the side of the road, glanced at my mother-in-law, and headed over the embankment.

Source: Jones, Sevilla, and Velman, _Disorderly Conduct: Verbatim Excerpts from Actual Court Cases_, New York: Norton, 1987.

The Transformed Tennis Player

Renee was a tennis player who had previously played on the men's professional tour. Following a sex change operation, she began to play on the women's professional tour and enjoyed a successful career as a female tennis player. When she entered to play in the women's U.S. Open, the tournament organizers decided to institute a chromosome test as a qualification for playing in the tournament. Renee could not, of course, pass this test even though she had all the sexual characteristics of a woman, with the exception of the ability to bear children. Renee claimed that the chromosome test violated her civil rights and that she was legally a female, and therefore eligible to participate in the tournament. Renee asked the court to grant an injunction preventing the tournament organizers from administering the test. The court permitted Renee to play because such a chromosome test is unfair, discriminatory, and inequitable; the test concentrates on only one factor in ascertaining sex and does not allow consideration of other factors.

Source: Hobbie, *World's Wackiest Lawsuits,* New York: Sterling Publishing Company, 1992.

The Drunk Painter

Tom, a painter, finished a job and had one and one-half beers with the owner of the house he was painting. While driving home, Tom was stopped by a police officer who requested a breath analysis. After complying, Tom was arrested for drunk driving for having a blood alcohol content of .20 percent, twice the legal limit. It was later discovered that the breath analysis machine misread paint fumes in Tom's breath as alcohol! Consequently, Tom was not charged.

Source: Head and Joye, *101 Ways to Avoid a Drunk Driving Conviction,* Atlanta: Maximar Publishing, 1991.

Indefensible Defenses

Although you might think defendants have their own best interests at heart, the following court excerpts show that some would have done better saying nothing at all.

THE COURT: The charge here is theft of frozen chickens. Are you the defendant, sir?
DEFENDANT: No sir, I'm the guy who stole the chickens.

THE COURT: You've been charged with armed robbery. Do you want the court to appoint a lawyer to represent you?
DEFENDANT: You don't have to appoint a very good lawyer, I'm going to plead guilty.

DEFENSE COUNSEL: Are you sure you did not enter the Seven-Eleven on 40th and N.E. Broadway and hold up the cashier on June 17 of this year?
DEFENDANT: I'm pretty sure.

The defendant, charged with arson, missed a court appearance.

THE COURT: Where were you?
DEFENDANT: In the hospital.
THE COURT: Why?
DEFENDANT: Smoke inhalation.

Source: Jones, Sevilla, and Velmen, *Disorderly Conduct: Verbatim Excerpts from Actual Court Cases,* New York: Norton, 1987.

The Testimony of a Ghost

In 1897, a man was convicted of murder based on the testimony of a ghost. In Greenbrier, West Virginia, a young bride of only two months died without anyone witnessing her death. Her new husband claimed he had come home and found his wife's body at the bottom of the stairs. Bystanders noticed that he did not allow anyone near the corpse. The bride's mother, who doubted that her daughter died an accidental death, went to the authorities and told them that her daughter's ghost appeared to her four nights in a row and described how her husband brutally killed her. Based on the mother's story, the bride's body was exhumed, and it was discovered that she died of a broken neck. Her husband was subsequently charged with murder. The husband was his own worst witness when he contradicted testimony and gave irrelevant details about his alibi. Although admitted as circumstantial evidence, the jury was impressed with the ghost story. After about an hour of deliberation the jury returned a verdict of first degree murder against the husband, who was sentenced to life imprisonment.

Source: Wallace, Wallechinsky and Wallace, *Significa*, New York: E. P. Dutton, 1983.

An Irate Taxpayer

Mike received his property-tax bill only days before his payment was due. To vent his frustration, he enclosed his payment in the envelope and wrote "Bob Wade, Bastard" instead of "Bob Wade, County Treasurer." In addition, on the memo line of the check, Mike jotted down an obscene message.

As a tax collector, Wade was used to a certain amount of resentment, but not to foul language. As a result, Wade filed a libel suit against Mike. Although the defendant argued that public officials should be able to take a little ribbing every once in a while, the judge did not agree and fined Mike double what he paid in taxes.

Source: Hobbie, *World's Wackiest Lawsuits*, New York, Sterling Publishing Company, 1992.

A Prostitute's Best Client

Scott believed prostitution should be legal and decided to go to court to defend his "right to sex." He sued his state claiming it was unconstitutional to have a law against prostitution because the state was forcing him to either abstain from sex or become a criminal to get sex. He reasoned that the state should have no jurisdiction in what was a natural act. After one court dismissed his case, he appealed to another court. The appeals court ruled that his case was frivolous and had no merit and penalized him with double costs and attorneys' fees.

Source: Ibid

Rear-End Trouble

When Brian saw Helene at PJ's, a university bar, he was so enamored by the attractive girl's shapely appearance that he grabbed her by the hips and gave her a bite on her buttocks. Helene was infuriated and bit back by suing Brian. She claimed that Brian, an attorney, should have known better. Brian responded that he meant the act as a compliment.

Helene's attorney stated that the bite broke the skin on her rear-end and caused "throbbing pain." Helene was forced to miss classes because she was unable to sit down for three days. Although Brian and his lawyer argued that Helene was only entitled to the $9 she spent on medication, the jurors awarded her $27,500!

Source: Ibid.

The Drowning Canoe

Marty rented a canoe from RJ and went out on the lake to enjoy a beautiful day. The canoe overturned, and Marty called for help. RJ heard the calls but ignored them, and Marty drowned. Marty's estate sued RJ. Believe it or not, the court ruled that Marty's estate could not collect damages from RJ because there is no duty to rescue under common law, the law based on prior court rulings.

Source: LaVallient and Theroux, *What's the Verdict?* New York: Sterling Publishing Company, 1991.

The Joys of Living on a Golf Course

Bruce and his family resided in a home next to a golf course owned by the city. The house was fifty yards from the green of a par three hole. As a result, his property was constantly pelted with duffed shots. After suffering twenty-two dents in the family cars, three shattered automobile windshields, and seven broken windows in the house and garage, he sued the city. Bruce succeeded in his suit and was awarded $2,500 for property damage and $3,700 for disruption of privacy. The judge, however, refused to rule that the golf course was a public nuisance, so slices and hooks continued to barrage Bruce's property. Bruce then attempted to file criminal charges against the city for 1,087 counts of criminal trespass and 1,087 counts of reckless endangerment by golf balls and people—one count for each golf ball in the family's four-year collection. Unfortunately for Bruce, the court ruled that he went over the boundary line on this claim.

Source: Hobbie, World's Wackiest Lawsuits, New York: Sterling
Publishing Company, 1992.

A Confused Judge

A judge in a Florida county court was in a legal quandary and hunting for relevant case law when two estranged homosexuals became embroiled in a legal dispute over who got to keep certain personal property after the pair split up. After meeting in a gay bar, the men dated a few times, hit it off and later moved in together. The plaintiff sued the defendant after a bitter breakup and months of bickering. It should have been an easy case for a judge to decide, but there was a problem because Florida does not recognize common law marriages, let alone homosexual marriages. Although gay-rights activists and other legal scholars were hoping this would be a test case for law relating to homosexual relationships, the parties came to their senses and settled the case through mediation.

Source: The Orlando Sentinel, June 20, 1993, page B1.

The Terrible Sports Fan

Mike was a big tennis fan, but he despised John McEnroe. When Mike attended the U.S. Open tournament in New York, he expressed his sentiments by cheering against McEnroe. He not only rooted for McEnroe's opponent, but he cheered each time McEnroe faulted. Visibly upset by this poor behavior, McEnroe exclaimed, "Don't you have anything better to do than cheer for my opponent all afternoon?" Mike replied, "No."

McEnroe shouted back an obscenity, launched into a verbal tirade, and threw his racket into the air, causing rosin from his grip to permeate the air. Then he resumed play and dispatched his opponent.

Days after the match, Mike filed a lawsuit against McEnroe, claiming he suffered "grievous physical and mental injuries." In deciding on the case, the judge found that, although McEnroe's conduct was "childlike," it was not intolerable. In dismissing the case, the judge decided that this conduct did not cause physical and emotional harm, and the worst Mike had suffered was a fleck or two of rosin drifting in his direction.

Source: Hobbie, *World's Wackiest Lawsuits,* New York: Sterling Publishing Company, 1992.

The Lottery Loser

Chrissy played the state lottery games religiously and finally was lucky enough to earn a spot on the weekly show to "Spin for $3,000,000." In a live telecast, Chrissy spun the wheel and watched in amazement as the wheel landed on her number, entitling her to the $3,000,000. The announcer shrieked, "You're a winner!" and the lights flashed.

However, moments later, the announcer tapped her on the shoulder and informed her that she was not a winner after all. The wheel had not remained on the slot for the required five seconds, and all bets were off.

The state lottery commission sent Chrissy a consolation check for $10,000, but she refused to give up her $3,000,000 without a fight. She sued the state lottery. During the trial, the jury reviewed the videotape of her spin and compared it with the spins of other winners. The jury decided that the state had not enforced the five second rule in the past, and there was no reason that the rule should be enforced now. Chrissy was awarded the $3,000,000 along with another $400,000 for emotional distress.

Source: Ibid.

Sober Plea

A female rock singer promised a judge that she would quit drinking alcohol after pleading guilty to pointing a shotgun at police officers during a drunken rage. Under a plea bargain, the singer agreed to attend three months of Alcoholics Anonymous meetings, perform 200 hours of community service, submit to random drug testing, and abstain from alcohol.

Source: *The Orlando Sentinel*, June 8, 1994, page A2.

The Suicide Pact

Leon and Michael were troubled young men who made a suicide pact. To carry out the pact, Leon drove his car over a cliff with Michael as his passenger. Michael died, but Leon survived the crash. Leon was charged with murder, but the court found him not guilty because this pact was really a double attempted suicide. The court ruled that he was guilty of attempted suicide, but not murder.

Source: LaVallient and Theroux, *What's the Verdict?* New York: Sterling Publishing Company, 1991.

The Invisible Gun

Steve robbed a woman in a parking lot while jabbing his hand in his pocket and pretending he was concealing a gun. The woman believed Steve had a gun and gave him her purse and jewelry. Steve was charged with first degree robbery, but avoided conviction because he did not actually hold a weapon. The judge ruled that the language of the law leads to the inescapable conclusion that actual possession of a weapon is a requirement for a conviction of the crime.

Source: Ibid.

What I Meant to Say Was

What would court records be without malapropisms? Here are a few misstatements from court transcripts:

Although somewhat large for his age, Tony appears somewhat smaller than he actually is.

He indicated his marriage was happy, as he and his wife have always been sexually combatible.

Defendant has been a crook all his life and is still in the restaurant business.

Subject owes no one but the finance company for his car and his mother.

The man died, but he went to court and beat the case anyway.

Source: Jones, Sevilla, and Velmen, *Disorderly Conduct: Verbatim Experts from Actual Court Cases*, New York: Norton, 1987.

Chapter 5

COMMON MISCONCEPTIONS ABOUT THE LAW

Interpretation of the law can be difficult even for the courts and the most skilled lawyers. No wonder laymen have so many misconceptions about what they think the law is. This chapter includes some of the most common misconceptions about laws in the United States.

Filing for Bankruptcy Discharges All Debts

Many individuals believe that they can be relieved of all debts by filing a petition for bankruptcy. This is not true. Although the goal of every debtor is to obtain a discharge releasing him or her of all debts incurred prior to the filing of a bankruptcy petition, debts such as alimony, child support, certain tax claims, and most student loans cannot be discharged by filing a bankruptcy petition. In addition, the filing of a bankruptcy petition does not release a person from claims for punitive damages from "malicious or wanton" acts such as drunk driving, which are penalties inflicted by courts. Also debtors going on a spending binge immediately prior to filing bankruptcy cannot discharge these debts if (1) the purchase totals more than $500; (2) it was payable to a single creditor; (3) the money was spent on luxury goods or services; and (4) the debt was incurred within forty days before the bankruptcy was entered. Furthermore, people contemplating bankruptcy should be aware that lenders and other credit sources may deny credit in the future, and credit reporting agencies may report bankruptcy on a person's credit report for ten years. These measures may cause the inability to procure a credit card, car loan, or mortgage for a home.

It Is Illegal to Marry a First Cousin

If you fall in love with your first cousin, you may be able to marry him or her, depending on where you live. The following states permit marriages between first cousins:

Alabama, California, Colorado, Connecticut, Delaware, Florida, Georgia, Hawaii, Massachusetts, New Jersey, New Mexico, New York, North Carolina, Rhode Island, South Carolina, Tennessee, Texas, Vermont, and Virginia. The District of Columbia also permits marriages between first cousins.

No state allows a marriage of a brother and sister, parent and child, uncle and niece, or aunt and nephew based on the incestuous nature of such marriages. However, a few foreign countries, including Russia and Italy, permit uncle-niece and aunt-nephew marriages.

Bigamy Is Permitted in Certain States

For those of you who think you can move to another state to have more than one spouse, think again. Bigamy—marriage to more than one spouse—is forbidden in all fifty states.

A Person Can Marry a Spouse of the Same Sex

Marriages between spouses of the same sex are not permitted in any state in the United States. In cases that have arisen challenging a state's prohibition, the courts have ruled that marriages between the same sex are prohibited because the marriage relationship has always been the union of a man and a woman as husband and wife, so no valid marriage contract entered into between persons of the same sex can exist. Some courts have gone so far as to rule that transsexuals cannot marry individuals of their former sex.

Murderers Not Caught for a Certain Period of Time Cannot Be Charged

No state has a statute of limitations for murder. A statute of limitations is a law that says no action can be brought after a certain period of time. Because no state has a statute of limitations for murder, a person can be charged with murder anytime in his or her life. Foreign countries also do not have statutes of limitations for murder, as evidenced by the prosecution of Nazi war criminals more than forty years after they committed wartime atrocities.

Public Laws Are Enforceable on Private Property

Lost item signs and traffic signs are not always enforceable on private property. For example, traffic signs in a parking lot that prohibit driving over a certain speed or making a right or left turn onto a public street or highway may not be enforced by a court. Courts have ruled that a person violating such signs is negligent and a contributing cause of an accident occurring as a result of such disobedience. If you have ever been involved in an accident on private property, you know that police officers cannot issue traffic citations for accidents or other violations occurring on private property. Also, signs stating that the property owner is not liable for stolen goods may not be enforceable in court, depending on the duty the property owner owed to the victim.

A Store Can Charge Its Customers Any Amount for Bounced Checks

The passing of a bad check can be a misdemeanor or felony in most jurisdictions, depending on the amount of the check. In Ohio, for instance, passing a bad check ranges from a misdemeanor of the first degree to a felony of the second degree, depending on the amount of the check and whether the individual passing the bad check has previously been convicted of other theft offenses. Regardless of the classification of the crime, most state laws limit stores in the amount they can charge customers for bounced checks. Many states have enacted deceptive trade practices laws that only permit a store to charge a specific amount for bounced checks. For example, under the Texas Deceptive Trade Practices Act, a store can charge a customer $15 for a returned check. A store can charge a customer more for a returned check only if the fee is reasonable, and it is agreed to in writing.

A Person Losing a Bank Debit Card Is Responsible Only for a $50 Fee

If a bank card is lost or stolen, the liability of the owner depends on how quickly he or she reports the loss to the institution that issued the card. Under the Electronic Fund Transfer Act, an owner's liability for a lost or stolen bank card is limited to $50 if the owner of the card reports the loss within two business days of the loss. If the owner waits, the owner is liable for the amount of charges up to $500 if the loss is reported within sixty days after the owner's bank statement is mailed. If the loss is not reported for sixty days after the owner's bank statement is mailed, the owner is responsible for all charges made after sixty days, even if these losses are greater than $500. A person failing to report a lost or stolen card can lose all the money in his or her account, along with any overdraft protection supplied by the financial institution. Therefore, if you lose a bank card, make sure that you report the loss immediately.

A Creditor Can Garnish a Debtor's Wages for a Debt Owed

In most states, a creditor can garnish a portion of a debtor's wages for a debt owed only after following certain procedures, including obtaining a court order. Most states have formulas setting forth the amount of each paycheck that a creditor can garnish to collect for a debt owed. In a few states, however, a creditor cannot garnish a person's wages unless the debt owed is for child support or taxes.

A Person Cannot Prevent a Debt Collector from Making Harassing Telephone Calls

Debtors who have creditors calling them may have some protection. Under the federal Fair Debt Collection Practices Act and similar debt collection acts enacted in most states, debt collectors are limited in their collection activities. The federal law makes it illegal for debt collectors to engage in any conduct designed to harass or abuse a person owing a debt. It is specifically illegal to cause a telephone to ring repeatedly with intent to annoy, abuse, or harass. It is also illegal to call without giving the caller's identity or to call before 8 a.m. or after 9 p.m. The federal law also states that when a debtor notifies the debt collector, in writing, that the debtor wants the collector to stop communications, the collector must stop all communications except advising the debtor of the collector's next step.

It is important to know that the federal law, as well as many state laws, only applies to debt collectors in the business of collecting debts for other people; they do not apply to creditors collecting their own debts.

Purchases from a Door-to-Door Sales Representative Cannot Be Returned

Those who are prey to door-to-door salespersons should be aware of the "cooling-off period." Both federal law and home solicitation acts enacted in many states give purchasers from door-to-door merchants a three-day cooling-off period to change their minds. Never pay cash in this situation because it is difficult to get a refund.

If you do pay with cash, contact the company directly and demand a refund. If your demand is refused, file a complaint in small claims court. If you pay by check, go to your bank and stop payment on the check. If you used a credit card, call the

institution that issued the credit card; tell them you are not paying the bill; and explain why. If these remedies fail, contact the
district attorney's office and the state attorney general's office
and report the company and the salesperson. The Home
Solicitation Act enacted in California, Florida, Michigan, New
York, and other states requires all door-to-door salespersons to
provide a notice of cancellation form on the contract signed by
the buyer. In certain cases, the federal Deceptive Trade
Practices Act will grant you substantial damages from the company and salesperson.

When Chasing a Law Violator, a State Trooper (County Sheriff, etc.) Is Prohibited from Crossing the State Line

Most states have extradition laws permitting law enforcement officers to cross state lines to pursue a violator of its laws.
This myth has been enhanced by movie chase scenes in which
a convict outraces a state trooper to the state boundary to avoid
prosecution. In addition, courts have stated that a trooper in
"hot pursuit" of a suspect can follow the suspect across state
boundaries.

A Ceremony Must Be Conducted to Marry Two People

Many states recognize common law marriages as legal and
binding marriages despite the lack of a formal ceremony. To
determine the validity of a common law marriage, the couple

must meet the following criteria: be competent to marry, have a present mutual agreement to marry, cohabitate, hold each other out as husband and wife, and be regarded and treated as husband and wife in the community. A person claiming common law marriage must prove the preceding elements with clear and convincing evidence.

State and Federal Deceptive Trade Practices Acts

Every state and the District of Columbia have enacted at east one statute with broad applicability to most consumer transactions aimed at preventing consumer deception and abuse in the marketplace. Many state statutes are patterned after the Federal Trade Commission Act, which prohibits "unfair or deceptive acts or practices." Most lawmakers and courts are careful to guarantee that these statutes are broad and flexible so that they can apply to creative new forms of business schemes in consumer transactions.

Almost all the state deceptive trade act statutes allow private actions for damages and award attorneys' fees for a successful plaintiff. In addition, these statutes grant a prevailing plaintiff certain penalty awards.

These statutes provide remedies against numerous deceptive acts including most sales to consumers, advertising, debt collection activities, lending, and automobile repairs.

By Getting a Product Patented, the Owner Has the Best Protection to Prevent the Competition from Copying It

Although a patent provides a monopoly that lasts for seventeen years, a good secret can last forever. Had Coca-Cola's formula been patented, for example, it would have expired years ago. By keeping the recipe a secret, Coca-Cola has been able to enjoy its exclusivity for many more years. Bear in mind, however, that keeping a secret can be very difficult.

As Long as You Don't Sell the Copies, It Is Legal to Photocopy a Copyrighted Work

This is deemed copyright infringement, although many people frequently do make copies of such copyrighted works. It is difficult for a copyright owner to police such violations, and the responsibility for policing infringement activities is the copyright owner's, not the copyright office's.

A Person Has the Right to Use His Surname as His or Her Trademark

Generally, this is true, but if a surname is already used as a trademark by a company and the public associates it with the products of that company, then a later user is an infringer because his use might deceive the public. For example, if two brothers with the surname of Brooks decided to open a men's clothing store, they would be denied the right to use the name

Brooks Brothers. Likewise, if your surname is Pepper, and you happen to be a doctor, you might have to choose another name for your newly formed soft drink company rather than calling it Dr. Pepper.

The Opening of a Bank Account in the Names of More Than One Person Entitles the Survivor of the Account Holders to the Balance of the Bank Account

Individuals opening joint bank accounts should discuss their intentions with their bank officer and read their bank account agreement. A few different types of joint accounts exist. One type of joint account has a joint tenancy with a right of survivorship, which entitles the sole survivor of the joint account holders to the entire proceeds of the account upon the death of the other account holders. A tenancy in common, on the other hand, does not contain survivorship rights. Other ownership forms of bank accounts do exist and should be discussed with an officer of your bank.

A Partner in a General or Limited Partnership Can Lose Only His or Her Investment, but No More

Distinct differences exist between a general partnership and a limited partnership. The differences between these entities rest in the liability of the individual partners. Most states have adopted the Uniform Partnership Act (UPA) and the Uniform Limited Partnership Act (ULPA), which govern general and limited partnerships, respectively. Under the UPA, all members of a general partnership share joint and several liability, which means that each partner may be held liable for the entire debts of the partnership, even if these debts exceed the partner's investment in the partnership. However, general partners in a general partnership have contribution rights, which allow them to pursue other partners for their respective portion of the debt, which is usually set forth in the partnership agreement. Under the ULPA, partners in limited partnerships are vested with limited liability and can only be held liable for their investment in the limited partnership.

A Taxpayer Can Give as Much Money as He Wants to Any Person Without Incurring Taxes

Under the federal gift and estate tax, all transfers in excess of $10,000 are taxable to the donor. This is bad news for those people who have a lot of money and are looking to get rid of some of it before they die to avoid federal estate taxes, which can amount to over fifty percent of an estate. However, under the current law, a donor can apply any gifts greater than $10,000 to his or her unified credit of $600,000 without incurring federal tax on the gift.

The federal gift and estate taxes are integrated into a single transfer tax under a unified rate schedule and unified credit. The gift tax is imposed on transfers during life, whereas the estate tax is imposed on transfers at death. Exemptions to the gift tax include all marital gifts (gifts from one spouse to another) and charitable gifts. The unified credit of $600,000 is allowed against the gift and estate taxes, permitting every donor to make gifts or bequests up to that amount without incurring the gift or estate taxes. A married couple can give gifts of up to $20,000 per donee without incurring any gift taxes. The value of such gifts or assets in an estate is determined by the price at which the property would change hands between a willing buyer and a willing seller, neither being under any compulsion to buy or sell, and both having reasonable knowledge of relevant facts (Internal Revenue Service Regulation 25.2512-1).

No Suits Can Be Filed Against a Person Involved in Bankruptcy Proceedings

It is true that the filing of a petition under various chapters of the Bankruptcy Code automatically "stays" (i.e., restrains) creditors from taking further action against the debtor, property of the debtor, or property of the estate to collect their claims or enforce their liens.

However, the Bankruptcy Code lists eleven types of actions not subject to the automatic stay, including criminal actions; the collection of alimony, maintenance, or support; governmental action; setoff of certain debts and an action for possession of non-residential property after the termination of a lease. In addition, a claimant can obtain relief from the automatic stay in certain situations to proceed against the debtor. Therefore, an individual contemplating filing a bankruptcy petition or suing a debtor who filed a bankruptcy petition should be aware of these exceptions.

An Oral Will Is Not Binding

A minority of states honor oral, or nuncupative, wills. These states include California, Illinois, Indiana, Kentucky, New York, and Ohio. Certain procedures must be followed for the will to be valid, including having witnesses who are not beneficiaries under the will and putting the words in writing within a certain time period after the communication occurs.

Minors Cannot Enter into Contracts

Minors can enter into contracts, but such contracts are voidable by the minor, which means that minors have the option of terminating the contract. People should be very careful when entering into contracts with youngsters because a minor can receive the benefits of a contract without the responsibilities. The only exception to this rule is that minors are bound by all contracts for necessities. The definition of necessity depends entirely on the person and the situation. For example, a minor entering into a contract to purchase listening tapes may be able to void the contract by enjoying listening to the tapes and not having to pay for the tapes. However, a court may require the minor to return all goods in his or her possession relating to the contract. Minority is one of many defenses to avoid a contract, including illegality, duress, fraud, and mistake.

A Person Bitten by a Dog Can Recover Damages from the Owner of the Dog

Many states have enacted "dog bite statutes," which state that if a dog does any damage to either the body or property of any person, the owner or keeper (or, if the owner or keeper is a minor, the parent or guardian of the minor) is liable for any resulting damages, unless at the time the damage was sustained, the injured person was trespassing; committing an illegal act; or teasing, tormenting, or abusing the dog. The owner or keeper (or the parent or guardian of the owner or keeper) has the burden of proving that the injured person was at fault for one of the reasons stated earlier.

An Engagement Ring Must Be Returned if the Engagement Is Broken

Courts have differed on this issue. A majority of courts follow the general principle that a man can recover the ring only if the engagement is dissolved by agreement or if the engagement is unjustifiably broken by the woman. The analysis in cases following this principle focuses on who is at "fault" for the termination of the relationship. The party to an engagement who was unjustifiably jilted becomes the owner of the ring as sort of a consolation prize. Some courts have found this theory sexist and archaic and hold that an engagement ring given in contemplation of marriage is a conditional gift, which becomes a completed gift only upon marriage. If the wedding is called off, for whatever reason, the gift is not a completed gift and must be returned to the man. State courts following this minority view include Iowa, New York, and Wisconsin.

A Homeowner Is Permitted to Shoot an Intruder

Courts rely on the facts of a case before deciding whether a homeowner violates the law by shooting an intruder. A homeowner must be acting in self-defense or protecting his property to be justified in shooting an intruder. Courts usually consider the amount of force used by the homeowner, which must be reasonable under the circumstances. If an intruder is in the process of leaving the scene of the crime, even though in the possession of stolen property, the homeowner cannot legally fire at him.

Under the First Amendment, a Person Can Say Anything He Wants at Any Time

Freedom of speech is not absolute. Although the First Amendment states, "Congress shall make no law . . . abridging the freedom of speech," the United States Supreme Court has held that the First Amendment is not an unlimited license to speak. As Justice Oliver Wendell Holmes, Jr., wrote in one of his famous opinions, the "most stringent protection of free speech would not protect a man in falsely shouting fire in a theater and causing a panic." In other decisions, the Supreme Court ruled that the federal government, along with local and state governments, can regulate certain types of speech, including the sale and distribution of pornography to protect public morals. The United States Supreme Court has set forth certain tests for the legality of pornography; however many cases still arise based on the differing opinions over what constitutes pornography. Former Justice Stewart stated, "I shall not today attempt further to define the kinds of material I understand to be embraced within [the words 'hard-core pornography'] . . . and perhaps I could never succeed in intelligibly doing so. But I know it when I see it . . ." People remain able to say almost anything against the government because the Supreme Court has continuously prevented the government from attempting to silence its critics.

A Landlord May Keep a Portion of a Tenant's Security Deposit for Ordinary Wear and Tear

A landlord cannot deduct damages from a tenant's security deposit for ordinary wear and tear. Most states have enacted security deposit laws; however, these statutes differ from state to state. Most security deposit laws grant a tenant multiple damages against a landlord violating the law, which include damages for double and triple the amount wrongfully withheld by the landlord. Some of these laws require a landlord to pay interest on security deposits greater than one month's rent, and other laws require a landlord to return a security deposit within thirty days after a tenant moves out or give written notice to the tenant as to why the deposit is being kept. In addition, these laws require tenants to follow certain procedures, including giving the landlord a forwarding address after moving from the premises. If your lease has expired and you gave your landlord a security deposit, check your state law to determine what rights, if any, you have against your landlord.

Neighbors Have No Recourse to Prevent a Dog from Barking

Everyone is annoyed by a neighbor's dog that barks outside all day. Many cities and counties have laws specifically relating to barking dogs. You may also be able to sue your neighbor for creating a nuisance. Most courts apply a test of whether a reasonable person would be seriously disturbed by the barking dog. If appropriate, you may want to call your local humane society to report the owner's inhumane treatment of the dog, especially if the owner keeps the dog outside all day in freezing temperatures. The humane society will advise you of local laws relating to cruelty to animals.

Small Claims Court Is Similar to Other Courts, but No Attorneys Are Involved

Most people are unaware of the benefits of small claims court. In many states, attorneys are permitted to appear on behalf of a party in a case in small claims court. In other states, lawyers can only represent a party if the other party agrees in writing.

Small Claims Court

The purpose of small claims court is to quickly resolve disputes involving small amounts of money, without long delays and formal rules of evidence. Examples of cases appropriate for small claims court include a landlord refusing to return a security deposit; a dry cleaner ruining a jacket and refusing to pay for it; and an uninsured motorist denting someone's fender. Small claims court differs from state to state and can have different names, such as "Justice of the Peace," "Conciliation," and "City" or "County" court. A person involved in a lawsuit in small claims court should consult the small claims court clerk for the local rules. Citizens should remember that their tax money pays for the court system, so they have the right to obtain information from the state about small claims court.

The following are three great advantages of small claims court:

1. You get to prepare and present your own case without having to pay a lawyer more than the claim is worth.

2. Bringing a dispute to small claims court is simple; very few legal forms are required.

3. Small claims court does not take a long time. Most disputes are heard in court within a month or two from the time the complaint is filed, and the hearing itself seldom takes more than fifteen minutes. The judge usually announces the court's decision either right in the courtroom, or mails it out within a few days.

The maximum dollar amount of a complaint brought in small claims court differs from state to state. The highest limit is in Tennessee, where a plaintiff can bring a suit for $10,000 (or $15,000 if the county has a population of greater than 700,000); the lowest dollar limit is Puerto Rico, where a suit cannot be initiated in small claims court for greater than $500. Most states have a dollar limit of between $1,000 and $2,000.

Sources: Warner, *Everybody's Guide to Small Claims Court*, Berkeley: Nolo Press, 1991; Rudy, *Small Claims Court: Making Your Way Through the System*, New York: Random House, 1990.

Public Schools May Teach Religious Holidays

The United States Supreme Court has ruled that public schools may not sponsor religious practices, but may teach about religion. The Supreme Court did not make a definitive ruling on religious holidays in the schools by upholding a lower court decision stating that the recognition of religious holidays may be constitutional if the purpose is to provide secular instruction about religious traditions rather than to promote the particular religion involved.

Source: "Religious Holidays in the Public Schools," a pamphlet sponsored jointly by American Academy of Religion, American Association of School Administrators, et al.

Contributing Sources:

Alderman, *Know Your Rights*. Houston: Gulf Publishing
Company, 1990.

American Bar Association, *You and the Law*. Chicago:
American Bar Association, 1991.

Belli and Wilkinson, *Everybody's Guide to the Law*. San Diego:
Harcourt Brace Jovanovich, 1986.

Coughlin, *Law for the Layman*. New York: Harper & Row,
1975.

Leeds, *Smart Questions to Ask Your Lawyer*. New York:
HarperCollins, 1992.

Sexton and Brandt, *How Free Are We?* New York: M. Evans,
1986.

Chapter 6

LEGAL WIT: QUOTATIONS BY AND ABOUT LAWYERS

One thing is certain, people like to talk about the law. In fact, throughout the ages and around the globe, the law has been a favorite topic of conversation. Consequently, law and lawyers are the subject of some wonderful quotes by some famous folks. You will recognize some of these words of wisdom, and others, while not familiar, are so apropos.

I learned law so well, the day I graduated I sued the college, won the case, and got my tuition back.
    FRED ALLEN

Some people think about sex all the time; some people think of sex some of the time; and some people never think about sex: they become lawyers.
WOODY ALLEN

America is the only country in the world where they let the prisoners go home and lock up the jury.
ANONYMOUS

Law is a bottomless pit.
JOHN ARBUTHNOT, M.D.

The law is reason free from passion.
ARISTOTLE

Even when laws have been written down, they ought not always to remain unaltered.
ARISTOTLE

Alimony is like buying oats for a dead horse.
ARTHUR BAER

If you laid all our laws end to end, there would be no end.
ARTHUR BAER

Laws are spider webs through which the big flies pass and the little ones get caught.
HONORÉ DE BALZAC

"Legally" is a robust adverb—it justifies many ill-gotten gains.
HONORÉ DE BALZAC

Getting kicked out of the American Bar Association is like getting kicked out of the Book-of-the-Month Club.
MELVIN BELLI, ON THE OCCASION OF HIS GETTING KICKED OUT OF THE AMERICAN BAR ASSOCIATION

Every law is an evil, for every law is an infraction of beauty.
JEREMY BENTHAM, *PRINCIPALS OF LEGISLATION*, 1789

The laws of a nation form the most instructive portion of its history.
EDWARD BIGGON

Laws are like sausages. It's better not to see them being made.
OTTO VON BISMARCK

Under our constitutional system, courts stand against any winds that blow as havens of refuge for those who might otherwise suffer because they are helpless, weak, outnumbered, or because they are non-conforming victims of prejudice and public excitement.
JUSTICE HUGO L. BLACK

It is far better that ten guilty persons escape than one innocent suffer.
SIR WILLIAM BLACKSTONE

Doctors and lawyers must go to school for years and years, often with little sleep and with great sacrifice to their first wives.
ROY G. BLOUNT, JR.

If nature had as many laws as the State, God Himself could not reign over it.
LUDWIG BOERNE

Crime is contagious. If a government becomes a lawbreaker, it breeds contempt for the law; it invites every man to become a law unto himself.
JUSTICE LOUIS D. BRANDEIS

The law is not an end in itself, nor does it provide ends. It is preeminently a means to serve what we think is right.
JUSTICE WILLIAM J. BRENNAN, JR.

A lawyer starts life giving $500 worth of law for $5, and ends giving $5 worth for $500.
ATTRIBUTED TO BENJAMIN H. BREWSTER

Society already understands that the criminal is not he who washes dirty linen in public, but he who dirties the linen.
VLADIMIR BUKOVSKY

Bad laws are the worst sort of tyranny.
EDMUND BURKE

Agree, for the law is costly.
WILLIAM CAMDEN

The law's final justification is in the good it does or fails to do to the society of a given place and time.
ALBERT CAMUS

'Tis easier to make some things legal than to make them legitimate.
SEBASTIEN CHAMFORT

When you have no basis for an argument, abuse the plaintiff.
CICERO

Who will protect the public when the police violate the law?
RAMSEY CLARK

Most people have come to recognize the law as the deadly enemy of justice.
DAVID CORT

When you go to court, you are putting your fate into the hands of twelve people who weren't smart enough to get out of jury duty.
NORM CROSBY

You can't have a constitutional right to do something that is illegal.
MARIO CUOMO

Lawyers and painters can soon change white to black.
DANISH PROVERB

The trouble with law is lawyers.
  CLARENCE DARROW

Nobody wants justice.
  ALAN DERSHOWITZ

A state is better governed which has but few laws, and those laws strictly observed.
  RENÉ DESCARTES

If there were no bad people, there would be no good lawyers.
  CHARLES DICKENS

"'If the law supposes that,' said Mr. Bumble, 'the law is a ass, a idiot.'"
  CHARLES DICKENS (FROM *OLIVER TWIST*)

When men are pure, laws are useless; when men are corrupt, laws are broken.
  BENJAMIN DISRAELI

Nor is the people's judgement always true;
The most may err as grossly as the few.
  JOHN DRYDEN

An appeal is when ye ask wan court to show its contempt for another court.
  FINLEY PETER DUNNE (MR. DOOLEY)

Every actual state is corrupt. Good men must not obey laws too well.
  RALPH WALDO EMERSON

The less government we have, the better—the fewer laws, and the less confided power.
  RALPH WALDO EMERSON

Some laws of state aimed at curbing crime are even more criminal.
  FRIEDRICH ENGELS

The most powerful seat at the negotiating table is at the head
of the table.
HENRY FORD

America, where, thanks to Congress, there are forty million
laws to enforce ten commandments.
ANATOLE FRANCE

The law is fair to all. In its fairness for equality it forbids the
rich as well as the poor to beg in the streets and to steal bread.
ANATOLE FRANCE

To some lawyers, all facts are created equal.
FELIX FRANKFURTER

Persons of good sense, I have since observed, seldom fall into
disputation, except lawyers, university men, and men of all
sorts that have been bred at Edinborough.
BENJAMIN FRANKLIN

God works wonders now and then;
Behold a lawyer, an honest man.
BENJAMIN FRANKLIN

Under current law, it is a crime for a private citizen to lie to a
government official, but not for the government official to lie to
the people.
DONALD M. FRASER

A good lawyer is a bad neighbor.
FRENCH PROVERB

A jury consists of twelve persons chosen to decide who has a
better lawyer.
ROBERT FROST

Be you never so high, the law is above you.
THOMAS FULLER

This won't be the first time I've arrested somebody and then built my case afterward.
    JAMES GARRISON

A lawyer and a wagon-wheel must be well greased.
    GERMAN PROVERB

No poet ever interpreted nature as freely as a lawyer interprets truth.
    JEAN GIRAUDOUX

You're an attorney. It's your duty to lie, conceal and distort everything, and slander everybody.
    JEAN GIRAUDOUX

There's no better way of exercising the imagination than the study of law.
    JEAN GIRAUDOUX

Laws are inherited like diseases.
    JOHANN WOLFGANG VON GOETHE

Lawyers are always more ready to get a man into troubles than out of them.
    OLIVER GOLDSMITH, *THE GOOD NATUR'D MAN*, 1768

The English laws punish vice; the Chinese laws do more, they reward virtue.
    OLIVER GOLDSMITH

A verbal contract isn't worth the paper it's written on.
    SAMUEL GOLDWYN

Divorce is a game played by lawyers.
    CARY GRANT

I know no method to secure the repeal of bad or obnoxious laws so effective as their stringent execution.
    ULYSSES S. GRANT, *ADDRESS*, 1869

Law is not justice, and a trial is not scientific inquiry into truth.
A trial is the resolution of a dispute.
    EDISON HAINES

The aim of law is the maximum gratification of the nervous
system of man.
    LEARNED HAND

I became a policeman because I wanted to be in the business
where the customer is always wrong.
    UNNAMED OFFICER QUOTED BY ARLENE HEATH

Fond of lawsuits, little wealth; fond of doctors, little health.
    HEBREW PROVERB

Order is the first requisite of liberty.
    GEORG WILHELM HEGEL

I'm not against the police; I'm just afraid of them.
    ALFRED HITCHCOCK

The life of the law has not been logic; it has been experience.
    OLIVER WENDELL HOLMES, JR.

Lawyers spend a great deal of their time shoveling smoke.
    OLIVER WENDELL HOLMES, JR.

When a legal distinction is determined . . . between night and
day, childhood and maturity, or any other extremes, a point
has to be fixed or a line has to be drawn . . . the line or point
seems arbitrary . . . but when it is seen that a line or point
there must be, and that there is no mathematical or logical way
of fixing it precisely, the decision of the legislature must be
accepted unless we can say that it is very wide of any reasonable mark.
    OLIVER WENDELL HOLMES, JR.

A man may as well open an oyster without a knife, as a
lawyer's mouth without a fee.
    BARTEN HOLYDAY

Brush Up on Your Shakespeare

One of the most famous quotes about the law is Shakespeare's "The first thing we do, let's kill all the lawyers." This quotation from *Henry VI*, Part 2, Act IV, Scene 2, has become quite popular and appears in bizarre places ranging from posters to bumper stickers to T-shirts—not where you'd ordinarily expect to find Shakespeare quoted. When taken out of context, it appears as though the bard of Avon has an aversion towards the law profession and wants to knock off all the lawyers.

Not true! On the contrary, in *Henry VI*, Part 2, the line is uttered by the contemptible Dick the Butcher, who suggests to Cade, an equally despicable character, that by getting rid of the barristers, bedlam and chaos would occur, and thereby support their conspiracy to overthrow the king.

So the next time you see this condescending quotation displayed in an effort to put down attorneys, kindly pass along the word that Shakespeare meant nothing of the sort.

There are a lot of mediocre judges and people and lawyers, and they are entitled to a little representation.
SENATOR ROMAN L. HRUSKA

Every once in a while you meet a fellow in some honorable walk of life that was once admitted to the bar.
KIN HUBBARD (ALSO KNOWN AS FRANK MCKINNEY HUBBARD)

The United States is the greatest law factory the world has
ever known.
    CHARLES EVANS HUGHES

There are not enough jails, not enough policemen, not enough
courts to enforce a law not supported by the people.
    HUBERT H. HUMPHREY

Lawyers earn a living by the sweat of their browbeating.
    JAMES G. HUNEKER

A shell for thee—And a shell for thee—but the oyster is the
lawyer's fee.
    THOMAS LEWIS INGRAM

Young lawyers attend the courts, not because they have business there but because they have no business anywhere else.
    WASHINGTON IRVING

That 150 lawyers should do business together is not to be
expected. [Referring to Congress]
    THOMAS JEFFERSON

The execution of the laws is more important than the
making of them.
    THOMAS JEFFERSON, LETTER 1789

Two farmers each claimed to own a certain cow. While one
pulled on its head and the other pulled on its tail, the cow was
milked by a lawyer.
    JEWISH PARABLE

A lawyer's relationship to justice and wisdom . . . is on par with
a piano tuner's relationship to a concert. He neither composes
the music, nor interprets it—he merely keeps the machinery
running.
    LUCILLE KALLEN, *INTRODUCING C. B. GREENFIELD*, 1979

I think we may class the lawyer in the natural history of monsters.

JOHN KEATS, LETTER TO GEORGE AND GEORGIANA KEATS, MARCH 13, 1819

Injustice anywhere is a threat to justice everywhere.

MARTIN LUTHER KING, JR.

The illegal we do immediately. The unconstitutional takes a little longer.

HENRY KISSINGER

The Supreme Court has handed down the Eleventh Commandment: "Thou shalt not, in thy classrooms, read the first ten."

FLETCHER KNEBEL

Screw the law—You get the guy off any way you can.

WILLIAM KUNSTLER

Lawyers, I suppose, were children once.

CHARLES LAMB

He is no lawyer who cannot take two sides.

CHARLES LAMB

The greater the number of laws and enactments, the more thieves and robbers there will be.

LAO-TZU

Those who uphold the law must be wiser and calmer than those who seek to repudiate it.

JOHN LINDSAY

The law is sort of hocus-pocus science, that smiles in yer face while it picks yer pocket.

CHARLES MACKLIN

A judge is a law student who marks his own examination papers.

H. L. MENCKEN

Injustice is relatively easy to bear; what stings is justice.
H. L. MENCKEN

A place where Jesus Christ and Judas Iscariot would be
equals, with the betting odds in favor of Judas. [Referring to a
courtroom]
H. L. MENCKEN

Ignorance of the law excuses no man from practicing it.
ADDISON MIZNER

There is no man so good, who, were he to submit all his
thoughts and actions to the laws would not deserve hanging
ten times in his life.
MONTAIGNE

There is no crueler form of tyranny than that which is perpetu-
ated under the shield of law and in the name of justice.
BARON DE MONTESQUIEU

I don't want a lawyer to tell me what I cannot do; I hire him to
tell me how to do what I want to do.
J. PIERPONT MORGAN

Laws not enforced cease to be laws, and rights not defended
may wither away.
THOMAS MORIARTY

In negotiations, always deal with the principal, not the agent.
GERALD L. NIERENBERG

We have to find ways to clear the courts of the endless stream
of "victimless crimes" that get in the way of serious consideration of serious crimes. There are more important matters for
highly skilled judges and prosecutors than minor traffic
offenses, loitering, and drunkenness.
RICHARD M. NIXON

In cross-examination, as in fishing, nothing is more ungainly than a fisherman pulled into the water by his catch.
    LOUIS NIZER

The people can change Congress, but only God can change the Supreme Court.
    GEORGE W. NORRIS

Laws were made to be broken.
    CHRISTOPHER NORTH (JOHN WILSON)

Where lawyers enter, tyranny begins.
    GREGORY NUNN

A contingency fee is an arrangement in which if you lose, your lawyer gets nothing—and if you win, you get nothing.
    GEORGE M. PALMER

It has been said that the course to be pursued by a lawyer was first to get on, second to get honor, and third to get honest.
    GEORGE M. PALMER

It was so cold one day last February that I saw a lawyer with his hands in his own pockets.
    ROBERT PETERSON

Law is nothing unless close behind it stands a warm living public opinion.
    WENDELL PHILLIPS

Where law ends, tyranny begins.
    WILLIAM PITT

Law school taught me one thing: how to take two situations that are exactly the same and show how they are different.
    ATTRIBUTED TO HART POMERANTZ

Law is experience developed by reason and applied continually to further experience.
    ROSCOE POUND

If you think that you can think about a thing, inextricably
attached to something else, without thinking of the thing it is
attached to, then you have a legal mind.
  THOMAS REED POWELL

The law itself follows gold.
  PROPERTIUS

Our very freedom is secure because we're a nation governed
by laws, not by men. We cannot as citizens pick and choose
the laws we will or will not obey.
  RONALD REAGAN

The minute you read something you can't understand, you can
almost be sure it was drawn up by a lawyer.
  WILL ROGERS

We want a Supreme Court which will do justice under the
Constitution—not over it. In our courts, we want a govern-
ment of laws and not of men.
  FRANKLIN DELANO ROOSEVELT

The decisions of the courts on economic and social questions
depend on their economic and social philosophy.
  THEODORE ROOSEVELT

Good laws lead to the making of better ones; bad ones bring
about worse. As soon as any man says of the affairs of the
State, "What does it matter to me?" the State may be given up
for lost.
  JEAN JACQUES ROUSSEAU

If the laws could speak for themselves, they would complain of
the lawyers.
  SIR GEORGE SAVILE

Ignorance of the law excuses no man.
  JOHN SELDON

Higher laws are unilaterally determined.
ERIC SEVAREID

The law hath not been dead, though it hath slept.
WILLIAM SHAKESPEARE, *MEASURE FOR MEASURE,*
ACT II, SCENE 2

He is always breaking the law. He broke the law when he was
born: his parents were not married.
GEORGE BERNARD SHAW, *MAJOR BARBARA*

Crime is only the retail department of what, in wholesale, we
call penal law.
GEORGE BERNARD SHAW

I'd like to get married because I like the idea of a man being
required by law to sleep with me every night.
CARRIE SNOW

Nobody has a more sacred obligation to obey the law than
those who make the law.
SOPHOCLES

He who goes to law for a sheep loses his cow.
SPANISH PROVERB

It is better to be a mouse in a cat's mouth than a man in a
lawyer's hands.
SPANISH PROVERB

Of course there's a different law for the rich and the poor;
otherwise, who would go into business?
E. RALPH STEWART

The law itself is on trial in every case as well as the cause
before it.
JUSTICE HARLAN F. STONE

While unconstitutional exercise of power by the executive and legislative branches is subject to judicial restraint, the only check upon our own exercise of power is our own sense of self-restraint.
   JUSTICE HARLAN F. STONE

The more numerous the laws, the more corrupt the state.
   TACITUS

Let him whose coat a court has taken, sing his song and go his way.
   THE TALMUD

Some circumstantial evidence is very strong, as when you find a trout in the milk.
   HENRY DAVID THOREAU

If law school is so hard to get through, how come there are so many lawyers.
   CALVIN TRILLIN

The law is a system that protects everybody who can afford to hire a good lawyer.
   MARK TWAIN

There is no end to the laws, and no beginning to the execution of them.
   MARK TWAIN

To succeed in other trades, capacity must be shown; in the law, concealment will do.
   MARK TWAIN

We have a criminal system which is superior to any in the world; and its efficiency is only marred by the difficulty of finding twelve men every day who don't know anything and can't read.
   MARK TWAIN

How to win a case in court: If the law is on your side, pound on the law; if the facts are on your side, pound on the facts; if neither is on your side, pound on the table.
UNKNOWN

Law school is the opposite of sex. Even when it's good it's lousy.
UNKNOWN

What do I care about the law? Hain't I got the power?
CORNELIUS VANDERBILT

Our court dockets are so crowded today it would be better to refer to it as the overdue process of the law.
BILL VAUGHAN

For certain people, after fifty, litigation takes the place of sex.
GORE VIDAL

I was never ruined but twice, once when I lost a lawsuit and once when I won one.
VOLTAIRE

Where the weak or oppressed assert the rights that have been so long denied them, those in power inevitably resist on the basis of the necessity for tranquility.
CHIEF JUSTICE EARL WARREN

Most good lawyers live well, work hard, and die poor.
DANIEL WEBSTER

It ain't no sin if you crack a few laws now and then, just so long as you don't break any.
MAE WEST

The law that will work is merely the summing up in legislative form of the moral judgement that the community has already reached.
WOODROW WILSON

It takes a whole lot of suits to keep a lawyer well dressed.
HENNY YOUNGMAN

A law firm is successful when it has more clients than partners.
HENNY YOUNGMAN

Laws of the Famous

BARNUM'S LAW: You can fool most of the people most of the time.

P. T. BARNUM

BERRA'S LAW: You can observe a lot just by watching.

YOGI BERRA

COOLIDGE'S LAW: Anytime you don't want anything, you get it.

CALVIN COOLIDGE

COOLIDGE'S SECOND LAW: A lost article invariably shows up after you replace it.

CALVIN COOLIDGE

CAUGHLIN'S LAW: Don't talk unless you can improve the silence.

LAURENCE C. CAUGHLIN

ETTORE'S LAW: The other line moves faster.

BARBARA ETTORE

GOMEZ'S LAW: If you don't throw it, they can't hit it.

LEFTY GOMEZ

LEC'S IMMUTABLE LAW: The first requisite for immortality is death.

STANISLAW J. LEC

LEVENSON'S LAW: No matter how well a toupee blends in back, it always looks like hell in front.

SAM LEVENSON

LEVENSON'S SECOND LAW: Insanity is hereditary—you can get it from your children.

SAM LEVENSON

LIPPMANN'S LAW: We all think alike, no one thinks very much.

WALTER LIPPMANN

POPE'S LAW: All looks yellow to a jaundiced eye.

ALEXANDER POPE

RUNYON'S LAW: The race is not always to the swift, nor the battle to the strong, but that's the way to bet.

DAMON RUNYON

TRUMAN'S LAW: If you can't convince them, confuse them.

HARRY S TRUMAN

TUCHMAN'S LAW: If power corrupts, weakness in the seat of power, with its constant necessity of deals and bribes and compromising arrangements, corrupts even more.

BARBARA TUCHMAN

Chapter 7

LAW TERMS EVERYONE CAN USE

This chapter includes common terms about the law that everyone should know. You're expected to know many of them, so don't think that just because you do, the terms included are too elementary—perhaps you're just a notch or two smarter than the average reader. Brush up on what you do not know because you never know when you may be confronted with some legal mumbo jumbo.

Keep score of your correct answers. If you score 70 or above, you probably belong on the Supreme Court of the United States. A score of 65 to 70 means that you're a law professor or a partner in a major law firm. A score of 60 to 65 means you've watched every episode of "L.A. Law" and/or are an associate in a law firm; and 55 to 60 means that you've been spending too much of your time with lawyers. Anything less than 55 means that you should thoroughly study this chapter because in today's world, your survival depends on it!

Acceleration

In the world of law, this term in a contract means that the full amount of debt you owe the other party must be paid after a certain event occurs (for example, missing a payment on a bank note gives the banker the right to make you pay the entire balance immediately).

Acquittal

When a person on trial gets an acquittal, he's off the hook. In the eyes of the court, he's innocent.

Affidavit

Most people have heard this term, but have no idea what it actually means. An affidavit is a sworn statement, usually signed by a notary. Affidavits are used by lawyers to get witnesses to swear to facts relating to an event.

As Is

"As is" means just the way you see it. Used items are often sold "as is," which means that a buyer gets a product just as he or she sees it, even if it breaks down the next day!

Bearer

A bearer is the person in possession of a check or other financial instrument. A check payable to bearer or endorsed without making it payable to any person is considered "bearer paper" and is therefore payable to anyone holding the check.

Bona Fide

This Latin phrase means in good faith, without fraud or deceit.

Breach

A "breach" occurs when a party to a contract breaks one of its promises under the contract. For example, a tenant breaches a lease by failing to pay rent when it is owed according to the lease.

Caveat Emptor

This phrase means a purchaser buys at his own risk. *Caveat emptor* translates as "Let the buyer beware." This is particularly important in real estate transactions; an inspection before purchasing property might uncover many defects not apparent at first glance, such as electrical problems, poor insulation, and environmental problems.

Check Kiting

This is an illegal scheme in which a false line of credit is established by the exchange of worthless checks between two banks.

Class Action

A class action refers to a lawsuit where a group of people institute a suit against one or more defendants. Class action lawsuits often occur in connection with plane crashes or train wrecks, where victims and bereaved family members join together to sue the airline, railroad company, or other party believed to be at fault.

Common Law

Common law is pre-colonial, unwritten law established by courts in England before law was created in the United States. Common law also refers to law derived from decisions of United States courts based on ancient custom and principles developed by English common law.

Consideration

Consideration refers to the value exchanged between parties to a contract. In a lease for property, the consideration given by the tenant is the rent, whereas the consideration given by the landlord is the use of the property.

Continuance

This is one of the few words in law that mean exactly what you think it means. A continuance is a court order that a hearing be postponed to a later date.

Counsel

If you do not know this one, you have had very few dealings with attorneys. Counsel is another word for lawyer or attorney. An attorney employed by a company to perform legal services on its behalf is said to be "counsel" for the company.

Covenant

Written promises in contracts are defined as covenants.

Creditor

A creditor is one to whom money is owed by a debtor.

Cross-examination

Cross-examination is the questioning of a witness called to testify by the opposing party. Commonly, a lawyer cross-examining a witness will ask only questions that can be answered "yes" or "no" to prevent the witness from explaining the answer.

Deed

A deed is a document that transfers an interest, generally in land, from a grantor to a grantee.

Defamation

This word means exactly what it sounds like—defamation is the act of hurting a person's "fame." Defamation is the publication of anything that injures the name or reputation of another or that brings disrepute to another. Written defamation is defined as libel; oral defamation is termed slander. Defamation itself is not a basis for a legal action; a plaintiff must base a complaint on either libel or slander.

The Difference Between Deeds

What's the difference between a quitclaim deed and a warranty deed? Both are signed documents that transfer property. A quitclaim deed transfers property "as is" and makes no warranties about the property. A warranty deed transfers good title to property free from any encumbrances, such as liens, leases, mortgages, easements, or taxes.

Default Judgment

A default judgment is a court decision given to a plaintiff (the person filing the lawsuit) when the defendant fails to respond to a lawsuit or show up in court.

Deposition

A lawyer has the right to question any person involved in a case prior to the trial. A deposition is the testimony of a witness under oath taken outside a courtroom and reduced to writing.

Doctrine

A doctrine is a government policy or principle of law that is not written in federal or state statutes, but nevertheless is widely accepted as a rule of law. An example of a doctrine is the Latin phrase "caveat emptor," which means "buyer beware" and applies to puchasers of real estate. Courts rely on this doctrine in requiring purchasers of real estate to beware of patent, or obvious, defects. Courts will usually only impose liability on sellers of real estate if defects are latent, or hidden, and the seller knew or should have known of a defect.

Domicile

This is a word used by lawyers to mean the place where a person has his principal home or place of business.

Double Jeopardy

Double jeopardy is a provision in the Fifth Amendment of the United States Constitution that prevents a criminal defendant from being prosecuted for the same crime more than once.

Dower/Curtesy

These are ancient words referring to the interest that a wife/husband has in a spouse's real estate. Frequently, dower/curtesy is defined as a life interest (a "life estate") in one-third of the real estate owned by the spouse at the time of death. Such an interest can be waived in most states. The majority of states have abolished dower and curtesy.

Draft

The legal term *draft* means an order for payment. A check is a draft because the person writing the check is ordering his or her bank to pay the amount of money specified on the check.

Easement

A right of one landowner to the use of the land of another, which is created by an express or implied agreement. This right of use cannot be inconsistent with existing uses of the land.

Encumbrance

An encumbrance is a third party's lawful interest in a person's property that creates a cloud on the title to such property. Encumbrances include not only liens such as mortgages and taxes, but also leases, water rights, easements, and other restrictions on the use of property.

Escrow

Escrow is an arrangement created by parties to a contract whereby a written instrument, such as a deed, is temporarily deposited with a neutral third party (called the "escrow agent"). The escrow agent holds the written instrument until the conditions of the contract are satisfied, at which time the escrow agent delivers the written instrument to the appropriate party pursuant to the terms of the contract.

Estoppel

The word *stop* hidden in the middle of this word gives a clue to its meaning. Estoppel is the inability to assert a right. Estoppel bars a person from denying the truth of a fact that has become settled by judicial or legislative proceedings. If a court estops a person from doing something, the person is not allowed to do it.

Et Al

These Latin words mean "and others." The name of a case is often referred to as Jane Doe v. John Roe, et al, which means Jane Doe sued John Roe and others.

Extradition

This is the surrender by one state to another of an accused or convicted person.

Foreclosure

The termination of a mortgage and the loss of possession of the mortgaged property is called "foreclosure." When a homeowner defaults on a mortgage, the mortgage is terminated, and the homeowner loses possession of the property.

Garnishment

Garnishment is the process in which money or goods in the hands of a debtor is taken to satisfy a debt. A plaintiff obtaining a money judgment against a defendant can garnish the defendant's wages or bank account.

Habeas Corpus

This is a Latin term that most people have heard, but few people actually know what it means. *Habeas corpus* is a court order requiring an officer who has custody of a prisoner to bring the prisoner before a judge to determine whether the prisoner has been unlawfully detained.

Hearsay

Hearsay evidence does not come from the personal knowledge of a witness, but instead comes from what the witness has heard others say.

Immunity

Immunity in a legal context means an exemption granted to one from a duty or penalty, which is contrary to the general rule. Witnesses are granted an immunity against self-incrimination—they do not have to answer any questions that would be considered an admission of their own guilt to a crime.

Indemnity

Indemnity is an agreement where one person promises to protect another person from loss or damage. Frequently, a commercial contract contains an indemnity clause in which one or both parties agrees to compensate the other party for the damage caused by the other.

Indictment

This is another word most people have heard or read in the newspaper, but few are sure what it means. An indictment is the determination by a grand jury that enough evidence exists against the accused to charge him or her with a crime.

Judgment

In the legal context, judgment is the decision of a court resolving the issues involved in a case.

Jurisdiction

A court's ability to hear and determine the merits of a case is called its jurisdiction. Without jurisdiction, a court's judgment has no legal force.

Laches

A lache is a lapse of time in enforcing a right of action and negligence in failing to act more promptly. A defendant to a lawsuit may rely on this legal theory to escape liability, because witnesses or evidence needed by the defendant to defend the "stale claim" may have become unavailable or lost due to the lapse of time.

Larceny

Larceny is a crime involving the unlawful taking of property with the intention of depriving the owner of its use. The felony crime of larceny includes embezzlement, obtaining property by false pretenses, acquiring lost property by any means, and issuing a bad check.

Lemon Law

This law has nothing to do with lemons and everything to do with cars, particularly bad cars. A lemon law is a law permitting the purchaser of a car to recover damages from the seller for deception or breach of a warranty. The name of this law is in reference to defective automobiles that, for years, have been called "lemons," a slang term.

Lien

A lien is a claim by a lender or other creditor on someone's property for some debt. To obtain a lien, a creditor must get a court judgment and then take proper steps to have the court file the judgment, which in some states is called a *certificate of judgment*. The creditor then must take the certificate of judgment to the county office where property deeds are recorded to establish a lien on the debtor's property. A mortgage is a lender's lien on a borrower's property.

Limited Liability

This is one of the few legal phrases defined exactly as it sounds. Limited liability is the limit placed on the amount an investor of an entity can lose resulting from a lawsuit against the entity. For example, in most circumstances, investors of corporations and limited partnerships can only lose the amount of their investment in such an entity.

Loan Sharking

This catchy phrase explains how certain lenders act like sharks in lending money at usurious, or exorbitant, interest rates. Most states have laws prohibiting loans with interest rates over a specified percentage. Loan sharking often arises in cases involving extortion, which is the threat to use violence to collect the interest or principal of a loan.

Mechanic's Lien

A mechanic's lien is a claim for payment by a mechanic or other contractor performing work on a property. In most states, this lien becomes a part of the county property records and creates a cloud on the owner's title of the property and the improvements on the property until payment is made or other circumstances occur.

Miranda Warning

This is the warning that must be administered to suspects prior to any questioning by law enforcement officers, that the person has the right to remain silent, that any statement he makes may be used as evidence against him, and that he has the right to the presence of an attorney, either retained by him or appointed by a court of law.

The Miranda Warning

The Miranda warning was created as a result of a 1966 United States Supreme Court case, Miranda v. Arizona. It began when Ernesto Miranda was arrested at his home and taken into custody to a Phoenix police station, where he was identified by a witness as the man who had kidnapped and raped another person.

Police officers took Mr. Miranda into an interrogation room and two hours later emerged with a written confession signed by Mr. Miranda that also stated that the confession was made voluntarily and "with full knowledge of my legal rights, understanding any statement I make may be used against me." The officers failed to advise Mr. Miranda that he had a right to have an attorney present.

The United States Supreme Court ruled that the confession could not be used as evidence of Mr. Miranda's guilt because it was not voluntary and that Mr. Miranda was not advised of his legal rights, which included the right to have an attorney present. The Fifth Amendment to the

United States Constitution states that no person can be compelled in a criminal case to be a witness against himself and no person can be deprived of life, liberty, or property, without due process of law. To ensure that other accused criminals are made aware of their constitutional rights, the Supreme Court ruled that a suspect who is taken into custody and interrogated must receive a warning of the following rights: the right to remain silent, that anything he says can be used against him in a court of law, that he has a right to the presence of an attorney, and that if he cannot afford an attorney, one will be appointed for him prior to any questioning if he so desires. The Miranda warning is now applied by law enforcement officers throughout the United States as a result of this ruling.

Mortgage

A mortgage is the document that transfers property rights from a debtor to a creditor as security for the repayment of a loan, which is usually part or all the purchase price of real estate.

Are You a Mortgagee or a Mortgagor?

A mortgagee (lender) lends money to a mortgagor (borrower) and takes a security interest in property owned by the mortgagor. A mortgagee is usually a bank or other lending institution, but can be an individual.

Negligence

This word is the basis for most personal injury cases. Negligence is defined as conduct that falls below the standard established by courts for the protection of others against unreasonable risk of harm. The standard used by courts is conduct that would be displayed by a reasonable person under similar circumstances. For example, if a motorist is charged with negligence in an automobile accident, a court must decide whether a reasonable person in the same situation would have acted in the same manner.

Non-recourse

Non-recourse means "without personal liability." A non-recourse mortgage means that a lender can only obtain the property subject to the mortgage if the borrower defaults and the lender cannot obtain money from the borrower. For example, if a borrower has a remaining balance of $50,000 on a non-recourse mortgage and the house is worth only $40,000, the borrower can only lose the house if he defaults. He will not have to pay the $10,000 difference between the mortgage and the value of the house.

Notary Public

This is an easy one—most people have used a notary public to witness the signing of certain documents. A notary public is a public officer authorized to administer oaths and to attest to and certify certain types of documents. The seal of a notary public makes a document authentic. In many states, lawyers are automatically eligible to become notary publics upon passing the bar examination. A "notario" in Spanish-speaking countries performs the same functions as an attorney. However, in the United States, a notary public is not permitted to perform the functions of an attorney.

Paralegal

A paralegal is a person other than an attorney who performs a variety of tasks associated with the practice of law that can be performed by a person not trained or authorized to practice as an attorney.

Parole

Parole is a conditional release from imprisonment that entitles the person to serve the remainder of the prison term outside prison if all the terms and conditions connected with the person's release are satisfied. Typical conditions of parole include periodic meetings with parole officers, no possession of weapons, and not associating with known criminals.

Per Annum

This means per year, or annually. Rent in a lease is often expressed as being owed per annum, which means rent owed each year.

Perjury

Perjury is the criminal offense of making untrue statements under oath. In some states, any false statements in a legal document or proceeding constitute perjury, even if the false statement is not important in a particular case.

Plea

A plea is a written statement that constitutes the plaintiff's (the person who initiated the lawsuit) allegation or a defendant's (the person against whom the lawsuit is brought) grounds for defense.

Power of Attorney

A power of attorney is an instrument authorizing one person to act as an agent on behalf of another.

Prenuptial Agreement

A prenuptial agreement (also known as an antenuptial agreement) is an agreement between two people who intend to get married that sets forth the rights of each person in the property of the other in the event of divorce or death.

Probate Court

Probate court is the special court handling the proceedings necessary to settle the estate of a deceased person.

Pro Bono

When attorneys handle cases without being paid, they are said to be representing their client *pro bono*. Literally, *pro bono* means "for the good."

Pro Se

Another Latin term, this means "for oneself." A person who appears *pro se* in a lawsuit is one who represents him- or herself without the aid of an attorney.

Restraining Order

A restraining order is an order handed down by a judge restraining or preventing someone from doing something. An example of a restraining order is when a person allegedly breaches a covenant not to compete with a former employer, and the employer obtains a restraining order from a judge preventing the person from competing until the merits of the case can be heard.

Retainer

A retainer is money paid in advance to a professional, such as an attorney, for future services to be performed. Some retainers represent the entire amount to be paid to an attorney for legal services; other retainers are merely a deposit for future services.

Statute of Limitations

This is the time period within which a lawsuit must be filed. It is normally figured from the date the act or omission giving rise to the lawsuit occurs, and it varies depending on the state and type of lawsuit. For example, the statute of limitations for a contract action may be fifteen years in one state and ten years in another state, whereas the statute of limitations for assault may be five years in one state and three years in another state.

Stipulation

A stipulation is an agreement to compromise a case entered into by the parties and presented to the judge. A stipulation often occurs when one party is willing to admit a formerly disputed fact.

Subpoena

A subpoena is a written court order requiring the person to whom it is addressed to appear in person in court to give testimony and/or to bring specific documents or other evidence. For example, subpoenas are issued to witnesses to crimes and require the witness to appear in court to testify about the crime.

Testator

A testator is the person who makes and signs a will. Historically, "testator" referred to a male, and "testatrix" described females; however, recently this distinction is no longer recognized, and both are described as a testator.

Tort

A tort is a personal injury for which a victim can file a lawsuit for damages based on the losses sustained by such injury.

What Is the Difference Between Assault and Battery?

Assault and battery are examples of torts. Both occur when a wrongdoer intends to inflict harm and imposes fear of injury on a victim.

Battery requires physical contact, whereas assault only requires a threat of physical contact.

Truth in Lending Act

This law requires a lender to give a borrower certain information relating to a loan, including a breakdown of the interest being paid over the life of the loan.

Unlawful Detainer

This is a legal term for eviction. It is also called "summary dispossess" or "forcible entry and detainer" in some states.

Usury

Usury is an exorbitant rate of interest. State statutes contain the maximum allowable interest rates that can be charged in a financial transaction. In many jurisdictions, a contract that includes a usurious rate of interest is unenforceable; in other jurisdictions, the borrower must return the principal portion of the loan.

Venue

In a legal context, venue is the locale for a trial. After jurisdiction is established, a trial can be moved within that jurisdiction for the convenience of the parties or to assure a fair trial.

Void

Void means having no legal force, unenforceable.

What Is the Difference Between a Void Contract and a Voidable Contract?

A void contract is one that may have the necessary terms, but is legally unenforceable. Void contracts include gambling contracts in states where gambling is illegal. A voidable contract is one that can be canceled by one party. Contracts with minors are voidable contracts that grant minors the right to cancel the contract unless the contract is for necessities, which include those things necessary to live, such as food and health items. However, the minor can ratify the contract once he/she is no longer a minor.

Voir Dire Examination

Voir dire is the examination of prospective jurors by a judge or attorneys to determine whether the jurors are qualified to sit on the jury for a particular case.

Chapter 8

SOME FREE ADVICE

In this chapter, nine lawyers who specialize in different fields   ranging from divorce law to labor law answer the following question: In your opinion as a specialist in your field, what is the single, most important thing the average person should know about the law?

These attorneys were chosen based on their extraordinary work in their field of practice and recognition among their peers. The nine attorneys are outstanding in their specialties, and as such, are paid substantial hourly fees. With this in mind, just one tip that you pick up from one of these experts will pay for the cost of this book twenty-fold or more. So read on, and enjoy—there's no time meter ticking away to distract you!

Estate Planning: Earl M. Colson on Wills

Arent Fox Kintner Plotkin & Kahn
1050 Connecticut Avenue, N.W.
Washington, D.C. 20036-5339

Do you have a will? The answer is "yes" whether you know it or not. All states have a statute that, in effect, serves as a will for those who fail to leave their own. Although they vary from state to state, these statutes typically provide for one-third of your assets to go to your spouse and two-thirds to go to your children. If you have no spouse, the children get it all. If you have neither children nor spouse, your property goes to other designated relatives.

If your state provides you with a will, why have your own? You need your own will for good reason: state statutes cannot meet your precise needs or follow your exact wishes. You may prefer to leave everything to your spouse, particularly if your children are young. And surely you would prefer to select an executor to carry out your wishes and a guardian to care for your minor children instead of leaving those important choices to a court.

Occasionally, people prepare adequate wills using forms available in a law school or county court library. However, if your assets are substantial or complex, an attorney can help you save on taxes and make sure that your will does what you intend.

Remember, one-size-fits-all clothing may look fine, but estate plans must almost always be custom made if they are to fit at all!

Domestic Relations: Susan M. Lach on Prenuptial Agreements

Lang, Pauly & Gregerson, Ltd.
4400 IDS Center
90 South Eighth Street
Minneapolis, MN 55402

A marriage is a legal contract between two people, sanctioned by the state. Therefore, because one out of every two marriages is dissolved sometime after the contract is made, it makes perfectly good sense to put into writing the specific terms of the contract. And if you don't do so, the state will do it for you upon the legal dissolution of your marriage.

A prenuptial agreement can help you avoid untold heartache and expense if it becomes necessary to end your marriage. This agreement can spell out your rights and responsibilities to each other during the marriage, or simply outline the terms and conditions of a fair division of property and debts in the event it should be terminated. It can be as simple or complex as you desire, and can be prepared alone or with the aid of an attorney.

The essential element is that both people make a complete disclosure of their assets and debts at the time of the agreement to be attached to the written document. After this is done, you can agree how these items should be divided in the event of a divorce. You also can agree how assets and debts acquired during the marriage should be divided. This portion of the agreement is particularly important for those entering into a second marriage who want to preserve their existing assets for their children from a prior marriage.

Most important, the two of you can put into writing the essentials of your marital "partnership." Will you both be employed outside the home? Will one of you give up schooling, a job, or career to raise a family? Is this an important contribution to the marriage recognized by both people? What do you anticipate will happen in the future (i.e., return to the work force or school for one, early retirement for the other)?

If you do not put these things in writing, the court will decide how to divide your property and debts and how to value your respective contributions to the marriage. Although many people feel that this advance planning takes away from the "romance" of marriage, preparing for the possibility of divorce when you are friends is infinitely preferable to leaving decisions in the hands of a stranger—an unknown judge—after the two of you are no longer able to have a friendly conversation.

Remember, everyone wishes you a long and happy marriage; few people can have a short and happy divorce!

Patents and Trademark Law: Frank H. Foster on Patents and Trademarks

Kremblas, Foster & Millard
7632 Slate Ridge Boulevard
Reynoldsburg, OH 43068-3126

Author of *Patents, Copyrights & Trademarks*
(John Wiley & Sons, 1993.)

With respect to inventions and patent law, do not sell, publish, or otherwise disclose your invention to the public until you have consulted with an attorney. Important patent rights can be lost because in most countries your right to a patent is destroyed if you make the invention public before you file a patent application. In the United States, you have a one-year grace period. Inventions can be disclosed in suitable circumstances, such as in connection with a confidential disclosure agreement. Consult first, or you may later find out that you have already destroyed important patent rights to things you have done. Some inventors learn this the hard way by losing their first invention in this manner.

Here are some other valuable tips: Do not deal with invention organizations that advertise for inventors in phone books, magazines, and on television, sometimes offering free invention kits. Do not overestimate the value of your invention. Do not fall for the old saying that if you build a better mousetrap, the world will beat a path to your door. Nothing could be farther from the truth. If you build the world's greatest mousetrap, you will still have to beat a path to the doors of the world. A commercially successful invention requires not only a good idea, but also competent business skills and capital investment. To succeed, an invention needs a coordinated business planning, manufacturing, marketing, and sales effort. Be realistic about royalties and expectations of financial reward.

With respect to trademarks, be aware that important trademark rights can be obtained by using a trademark commercially in connection with the sale of goods and services.

Registration is not a requirement for trademark rights, although it does strengthen them. However, forming a corporation and having it registered with a corporate name does nothing to ensure your right to use that corporate name prominently in connection with your business.

Do not select as a trademark words that describe your goods or services or some characteristic or feature of your goods or services. Although such terms can become trademarks, they can be the sources of expensive litigation. In general, the more generic a company's name, the more difficult it is to protect its trademark.

Litigation: Alan Farber on Lawsuits

1430 Grant Building
Pittsburgh, PA 15219

Avoid litigation. A lawsuit should be a last resort, to be pursued only after all other avenues have been exhausted.

Consider what your best alternative to a lawsuit is and then decide if you can reasonably expect to do any better at trial.

Litigation is a slow process that can easily last years before a trial date is reached. After you reach trial, you have no guarantee that a jury is going to find in your favor. Every story has two sides, and our legal system controls how both sides present their stories. You might be prevented from offering what you think is crucial information due to the rules of evidence.

Very rarely does a court award attorney fees to the "winner" of a lawsuit. Even if you are successful at trial and the jury awards you all the money you are claiming, you still must pay your attorney. Keeping this in mind, review your alternatives to a lawsuit, and only file a lawsuit after all else fails.

Franchising: Philip F. Zeidman on Franchising

Brownstein, Zeidman & Lore
1401 New York Avenue, N.W., Suite 900
Washington, D.C. 20005-2102

Whether you are a producer of goods or services looking for a better, faster, more profitable way to expand; a retail business owner looking to increase revenue; an independent retailer losing your market to large chains that can compete more effectively with mass advertising and purchasing; or an employee wanting to preserve your security, but at the same time gain the independence associated with owning your own business; franchising may be the answer. I emphasize "may" because franchising is not the right course for every person or business, and not necessarily the right course for a business during a particular stage of its development. But the sheer size and growth of franchising makes it an option hard to ignore. For example, another franchise opened every sixteen and one-half minutes somewhere in the United States in 1993, when franchises were responsible for 35 percent of total United States retail sales.

For the company that desires to expand its distribution, franchising can provide an opportunity to do so by leveraging the efforts and investments of others, while avoiding the cost and burden of hiring your own employees, establishing your own retail outlets, developing promotions, and other benefits provided by a franchisor.

For the existing retailer, franchising may enable you to expand by granting others the right to operate a business such as the one you've developed, using your proven concepts in return for a fee or other payment; or you may find that you will be better able to join the competition by converting your independent operation into a franchisee of a regional or national chain.

For the employee, you may find that franchising permits you to "own your own business" with much greater likelihood of success than simply establishing an independent operation because of the support and other benefits you receive from being a part of a franchised network.

It is important to remember the following points for successful franchising:

1. Unless the product or service can command an advantage over competitors, franchising does not ensure success.

2. Not every product or service or business lends itself to being franchised.

3. No matter how successful the franchise, continued success depends on hard work and personal qualities of the franchisee. Make sure that you know yourself well enough to know whether you can fit into the requirements of the franchise.

4. A wealth of information is available—but none more valuable than the experiences of other franchisees. It is well worth looking for answers if you believe you and your business fit into the franchise scenario.

Keep in mind that federal and state laws govern the offer and sale of franchises. In addition, the traditional principles of contract law apply to the franchise agreement. Finally, don't let yourself get hung up on the law first—don't let the legal tail wag the business dog. The decision of whether franchising is right for you and your business is, first and foremost, a business decision.

Entertainment and Sports Law/Negotiating: Robert G. Woolf on Negotiating

Bob Woolf Associates, Inc.
4575 Prudential Tower
Boston, MA 02199

Author of *Friendly Persuasion: How to Negotiate and Win* (G. P. Putnam's Sons, 1990) and *Behind Closed Doors* (Atheneum, 1976)

In my specialty area of sports law/negotiation, I have discovered that people are afraid of the actual process of negotiating. They are under the impression that you are not negotiating effectively unless you are shouting, banging the table with your fists, or totally intimidating your "opponent." Change that attitude!

A negotiation is an opportunity to persuade someone to adopt your point of view. Present yourself as someone who is going to work very hard to reach a mutually beneficial resolution. Shift the emphasis to an atmosphere of teamwork, rather than two warriors going into battle. By creating a friendly atmosphere, you can help ease the other side's tension and encourage them to open up more, thus giving you more information to work with during the negotiations.

One of the most important tenets of negotiating is this: Information is power. If you prepare properly, you can cull helpful pieces of information that can increase your leverage in any negotiation. For instance, if you are buying a house, you will certainly research comparable house sale prices in the area, but also see if you can find additional information about your prospective seller's history. How much did he/she pay for the house; is he/she in a cash flow bind; is he/she in a "must move" situation, and so on. In these instances, perhaps you could increase the cash down payment as opposed to increasing your actual price offer. The more information you have going into the negotiations, the more opportunity you will have to be creative and make the agreement more appealing to the other party. Remember, everything is negotiable.

In this age of global communication and business transactions, take special care to educate yourself on the customs and possible expectations of other cultures, so as not to offend inadvertently and derail your efforts and goals. For example, the Japanese usually answer "hai" (yes) to everything that you say to be polite; they do not mean that they are in agreement with you. Many hand gestures accepted in America, such as the "okay" sign have very insulting connotations in Egypt. The Chinese prefer not to be touched in any way or slapped on the back as we may do when first meeting or ending a meeting.

After you have properly prepared yourself with as much information as possible, concentrate on your style of presentation. Always speak in a clear and modulated tone; don't ever get angry or curse, even if others around you are doing it. You don't have to be disagreeable to disagree. If things are getting out of hand, end the meeting quickly and wait a few days to reschedule so that tempers have a chance to settle down. Never use confrontational words, such as "demand"; instead use "suggestion" or "proposal." Also never say, "take it or leave it" because most people will "leave it" just on principle. Say instead, "I am working with a difficult time frame, and I am hoping you will be able to accommodate my situation." I have found that when treated with respect and dignity, most people respond in kind, and nine out of ten negotiations will be successful for all parties involved and lead to future successful business dealings.

Real Estate: Judith D. Levine on Buying Real Estate

Hahn Loeser & Parks
One Columbus
10 West Broad Street, Suite 1800
Columbus, OH 43215

The largest single investment made by most people in a lifetime is the purchase of a home. The law requires that any contract for the purchase or sale of real estate must be in writing. Most home buyers draft the purchase contract themselves or with the aid of a broker. It is important to employ a lawyer who understands both your requirements and your objectives and has the ability to craft a contract that protects your interests.

The contract is the road map for your transaction. It should describe what each party will do. If you are purchasing a home, make sure that the contract lists everything you think you are getting. If you cannot purchase the home without financing, the contract and the performance of your obligations should be contingent upon your receiving financing satisfactory to you. The contract should allow you to make whatever inspections you feel are necessary in deciding whether to proceed with the purchase.

Although the custom varies in every community as to who (the buyer or the seller) pays for title insurance, every contract for the purchase of real estate, be it residential or commercial, should provide that the buyer will have title insurance coverage. Although most buyers receive a general warranty deed from the seller, there is no assurance that the seller will be financially able to compensate the buyer if a title defect exists. A title defect might be as minimal as a several-inch encroachment of a neighboring driveway or as serious as a forged deed in the chain of title. The title insurer will pay up to the total purchase price in the event of a complete loss of title.

Most important, the contract should describe the rights of each of the parties in the event one party does not perform. Don't be swayed even if the other party is your best friend. The contract is for the time when all does not go well, and the other party is no longer your friend.

Business Law: John C. Lightbody on Liability

Murray, Plumb & Murray
75 Pearl Street
Portland, ME 04101

Did you know that most owners of small businesses are subject to unlimited personal liability? Entrepreneurs and small business owners are personally responsible for each and every debt of the business, whether the debt is a simple account payable, a warranty claim, or a claim for personal injuries.

This unlimited liability occurs because the most common forms of business entity are sole proprietorships and general partnerships. If only one principal exists, a small business is more likely to be a sole proprietorship. If a small business has two or more principals, it is most likely to be a general partnership. A general partnership usually exists even if the relative ownership interests of the principals are different (even if one of the principals is only a one percent owner). No matter how big or small your ownership is in a general partnership, your liability is the same.

The potential risks and exposure business owners face from unlimited liability can be very small or significant, depending on the nature of each particular business; however, such unlimited exposure exists in every sole proprietorship and general partnership.

The risk of unlimited liability means that everyone involved as a principal in a business should pay careful attention to the form of that business enterprise. This applies to all owners of the business, including inactive or non-manager owners who provide only capital in exchange for a share of the earnings or profits. A proprietorship and general partnership are the forms of entity created automatically by law if the proper steps are not taken to create another form of entity—either a corporation or a limited partnership. The shareholders of a corporation and the limited partners of a limited partnership generally have limited liability, which means that an individual can only lose his or her investment in the business, unless certain formalities are not observed.

The form and structure of every new business should be examined at the outset. Principals should not simply ignore this issue and do nothing—even though that is the easiest and cheapest in the short run. Rather, the risk of exposure to claims resulting from the business should be examined and evaluated. A sole proprietorship or simple oral general partnership may be an adequate form of organization. However, the only way for principals who are active managers in the business to reduce their liability is to incorporate the business. The benefits of incorporation can be achieved only by preparing and filing the necessary papers with proper state authorities—generally the Secretary of State for that particular state—and by taking other necessary steps to create and maintain a corporation.

Employment Law: Melissa Zox-Feldman on Documenting Employee Relations

Schottenstein, Zox & Dunn
Huntington Center
41 South High Street, Suite 2600
Columbus, OH 43215

Although most employment relationships begin amicably, legal disputes do arise. To aid in pursuing or defending a labor or employment dispute before an administrative agency or a court, maintaining and presenting continuous and thorough documentation by both the employee and the employer is essential.

The paperwork trail should begin with a carefully prepared and completed employment application. The employer should create, with the assistance of legal counsel, an employment application informing the applicant that the application is not a contract of employment, and that the applicant, if hired, is free to resign at any time and can be terminated at any time with or without cause and with or without notice. This employment at-will language, or the absence thereof, is significant evidence in a wrongful discharge lawsuit brought by a former employee against his or her former employer. The employment application should also contain a statement that the applicant consents to lawful drug testing and post-offer medical examinations.

The employer must be certain that the application does not include any type of unlawful inquiries about an applicant's race, color, sex, age, national origin, handicap, disability, veteran's status, or any other state or federally protected category. Any questions about an applicant's disability must be limited to whether the applicant is aware of any disability preventing him or her from performing one of the primary functions of the job. In the event such a question is asked, the employer should provide the applicant with a detailed job description, noting the primary functions of the position. An applicant should carefully review and truthfully complete the employment application before signing it.

The employer should also distribute and abide by an Employee Handbook, prepared with the help of legal counsel. This well-drafted document provides performance guidelines to an employee and is drafted loosely enough to allow the employer flexibility in hiring, managing, disciplining, and terminating its employees. On the other hand, a poorly prepared handbook can be used by a former employee as a basis for a wrongful discharge lawsuit against his or her former employer. For the employer, a comprehensive at-will employment statement, signed by the employee in duplicate, is the most important policy in the handbook. The employee's copy should remain in the handbook, and the employer should retain a copy in the employee's personnel file.

Throughout the employment relationship, the employee and the employer should record the progression of the employment relationship. The employer should use standard forms for documenting all disciplinary actions. For example, the employer should utilize forms to record disciplinary incidents, verbal warnings, written warnings, suspensions, and terminations. The forms should require a written narrative of the incident. The employee should be requested to sign the form below a statement establishing that the employer reviewed the content of the form with the employee. If the employee refuses to sign, a witness should sign acknowledging that fact. It is recommended that the employee present his or her version of the incident on the form as well. Additionally, the employee should ask for a copy of the discipline form and maintain it with his or her records at home. Similarly, if the employee believes he or she may have a cause of action for discrimination or wrongful discharge, the employee should attempt to keep a daily diary noting any objectionable behavior or promises of employment for a definite period of time.

Performance evaluations, at the end of a training period, and then at least annually, also can provide helpful documentation for both parties. The evaluation should use an objective rating system within designated performance categories. Space should be available for written comments by the evaluator and the employee. The evaluator must be trained for the proper use of the performance appraisals. It is imperative that the evaluator honestly complete the evaluation, noting any particular performance deficiencies. Likewise, the employee should use the evaluation process as an opportunity to document and submit to the employer his or her own self-evaluation, or in the alternative, a rebuttal to the employer's evaluation. Thereby, once again, both parties are creating a record of the employment relationship that will be crucial in pursuing or defending a legal action. The evaluations must be reviewed with the employee, after which he or she should be requested to sign the appraisal. Again, if the employee refuses to sign the form, have a witness sign acknowledging that fact.

Documenting every aspect of an employment relationship is beneficial for all employees, irrespective of job position and all employers, irrespective of type or size of business. If an employment relationship turns sour, a record tracing an individual's employment and the employer's treatment of the employee, aids a lawyer in providing the employee or the employer with the best possible representation.

Although the preceding procedures seem time-consuming and complicated, careful application can curtail much grief down the road.

INDEX

199